Countdown to Christmas

Amy Puetz Fox

Memory Making Stories & Activities for Every Day from December 1st to the 25th

Golden Prairie Press

Countdown Books by Amy Puetz Fox

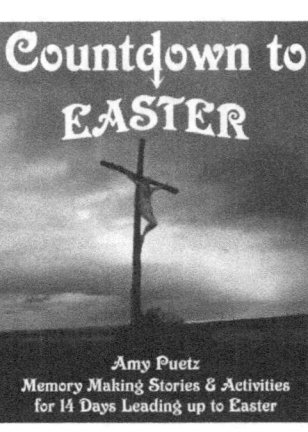

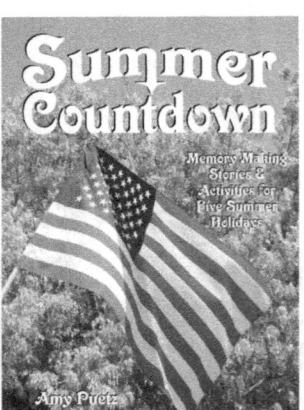

AVAILABLE AT WWW.GOLDENPRAIRIEPRESS.COM

To the One who was willing to be to born in a stable and die on a cross.
Thank you Jesus!

To my family!
For all the wonderful Christmas celebrations we have shared over the years.

Copyright 2010 by Amy Puetz Fox, revised 2022
All Rights Reserved.
No part of this book may be reproduced in any form or by any electronic or mechanical means including information storage and retrieval systems, without permission in writing from the author. The only exception is by a reviewer, who may quote short excerpts in a review.

Published by Golden Prairie Press
Gillette, Wyoming
Cover and Layout Design by Amy Puetz Fox

All of the quotes, poems, riddles, carols, and "classic" stories in this book where published before 1923 and are in the public domain. Even though the stories themselves are in the public domain this anthology is copyrighted.

ISBN: 978-0-9825199-1-2
LCCN: 2009938475
Library of Congress Cataloging-in-Publication Data
Includes index.
I. 1. Classic Stories. 2. Christmas—Crafts. 3. Christmas—Games. 4. Riddles. 5. Christmas Carols.
II. Title

Contents

Introduction..1
"A Merry Christmas" by Frances Ridley Havergal........2
December 1……………………………………….....3
"Becky's Christmas Dream" by Louisa May Alcott 4, "A Christmas Carol for Children"
by Martin Luther 6, Christmas Games—Blind-man's Buff and Hunt the Slipper 7
December 2………………………………....……...8
"The Fir-Tree" by Hans Christian Andersen 9, The Spirit of Christmas From *Pickwick Papers*
by Charles Dickens 13, Christmas Craft—Little Box Ornaments 14
December 3...16
"The Star" by Florence M. Kingsley 17, Christmas Quiz—In Other Words 19
December 4...20
"The Conscience-Pudding" Part 1 by E. Nesbit 21
Christmas Cooking—Plain Bread Pudding, Plum Pudding 25 and Vanilla Pudding 26
"Christmas: Blest Feast of the Nativity!" by W. F. D. 26
December 5...27
"The Conscience-Pudding" Part 2 by E. Nesbit 28, Christmas Chuckles 32
Christmas Carols—"O Come, All Ye Faithful" 33, "Hark! the Herald Angles Sing" 34
December 6...35
"Saint Nicholas" Adapted by Amy Puetz Fox from an original by Robert Chambers 36
Christmas Celebration in Other Countries 37
Christmas Games—Even or Odd? and Beans are Hot 38
December 7...39
"Why the Chimes Rang" by Raymond MacDonald Alden 40, Christmas Traditions—The Origin
of the Christmas Stocking 42, Riddles by Melville De Lancey Landon and Mark Twain 43
December 8...44
"Christmas Every Day" by W.D. Howells 45, "A Candlemas Dialogue" by Christina Rossetti 49
Christmas Craft—A Scrap-bag and A Walnut-shell Turtle 50
December 9...51
"Wenceslas" by Amy Puetz Fox 52, "A Christmas Greeting" 53, "Good King Wenceslas"
by John Mason Neale 54, Christmas Cooking—Fudge, Butterscotch, and Parisian Sweets 55
December 10...56
"Paulina's Christmas" by Anna Robinson 57, "Time Flies: A Reading Diary" by Christina Rossetti
59, Christmas Carols—"O Little Town of Bethlehem" 60 and "Joy to the World!" 61
December 11...62
"Christmas Storms and Sunshine" Part 1 by Elizabeth Gaskell 63
"A Christmas Carol" by Christina Rossetti 66 , Christmas Play 67
December 12...68
"Christmas Storms and Sunshine" Part 2 by Elizabeth Gaskell 69
The Word "Christmas—It's Orthography and Meaning by William Francis Dawson 72
Christmas Games—Puss in the Corner 72, and Earth, Air, Fire, and Water 73
December 13...74
"Christmas Far From Home" by Amy Puetz Fox 75
Christmas Newspaper 78, Newspaper Layout Pages 79–82

Contents

December 14...83
"Trusty's Christmas" by Carolyn Sherwin Bailey 84, The 12 Days of Christmas
by John Rodemeyer 87, Christmas Craft—Lanterns by Susie B. Wines 88

December 15...89
"A Story of the Christ-Child" A German Legend as told by Elizabeth Harkison 90
Christmas Carols—"Away in a Manger" 92 and "We Three Kings of Orient Are" 93

December 16...94
"Getting a Christmas for the Little Ones" by Margaret Sidney 95
Christmas Games—Buz and Musical Chairs 100

December 17..101
"Christmas Bells!" by Margaret Sidney 102, Quote from *Christmas Carol* 106
Christmas Carols—"Deck the Hall With Boughs of Holly" 107 and "Silent Night" 108

December 18..109
"The Legend of Babouscka" Adapted from a Russian Tale 110, "Love Came Down"
by Christina Rossetti 110, Christmas Craft—Picture-Frame, and Paper Chains 111
Remembering Those Far Away by Howard Roscoe Driggs 112
A Simple Bill of Fare for a Christmas Dinner by H.H. 113

December 19..115
"The First Christmas Tree" by Eugene Field 116, "While Shepherds Watched"
by Nahum Tate 118, Riddles by Melville De Lancey Landon, Mark Twain and Others 119

December 20..120
"The Shepherd's Story" Part 1 by Washington Gladden 121, Christmas Joy 123, Christmas Carols—
"I Heard the Bells on Christmas Day" 124 and "It Came Upon the Midnight Clear" 125

December 21..126
"The Shepherd's Story" Part 2 by Washington Gladden 127
"The Birth of Christ" by Alfred Tennyson 130
Christmas Cooking—Christmas Cookies, Frosting, and Gingerbread Men Cookies 131

December 22..132
"The Coming Messiah" From the Bible 133, "Christmas Day" by Christina Rossetti 134 Christmas
Games—How, When, and Where and Contradiction 135

December 23..136
"Birth of Jesus" From Matthew 1 137, "The Christmas Spirit" by Hugh Hume 138
Christmas Craft—Christmas Carol Wall Hanging 139

December 24..140
"The Christmas Story" From Luke 1 141, Christmas Quiz—Who Said It? 143

December 25..144
"Christ is Born" From Luke 2 145, Christmas Carols—"God Rest ye, Merry Gentlemen" 146
and "Oh Come, Oh Come, Emmanuel" 147

Index..148

Introduction

It is my sincere wish that this book will be used to create wonderful memories for you and your family. In our society there are so many things that vie for our attention that we often don't spend time with those we love most. A hundred years ago things were very different. Families spent time in the evenings talking, reading, singing, and just fellowshipping. With the creation of the radio things changed and when television became a staple in every home the interaction between family members decreased even more. Now with computers, movies, and a myriad of other gadgets, families spend very little time building relationships. This book has a mission to help families grow closer together.

Before you jump into this book I have a few things I'd like to say. The book is broken up into daily sections. Each day has a story and an activity that should take about 30 to 45 minutes. The story is first but feel free to change it around and start with the activity if it works best for you. Some of the activities (such as the cooking) may take more than the allotted time, so preview the activity before you get started. For instance on December 4th there are recipes for making two bread puddings and vanilla pudding. You might get the vanilla pudding started and while the children are stirring it you could read the story. Also if one of the activities doesn't sound like much fun, feel free to implement your own. If you have a special recipe you make every year, do this on one of the cooking days, or if you have a craft that you enjoy do that on a craft day.

Nearly all the stories in this book were written in the 1800s and early 1900s so some of the language may seem old fashioned. I have modernized some of the spelling but I left most of the stories intact because the Victorian people had such a beautiful way of using words. It is always good to stretch our own vocabulary. Many of these stories have not been reprinted since their first publication and I'm so excited to share these with a whole new generation. Most of the stories can be used to help teach children important lessons. At the end of each story you could think of a few questions to ask your children, or maybe even have the children ask you questions! For instance on December 1st you could ask, "What are some things that you really dislike doing, and how can you be cheerful about doing them anyway?" You could also have the children look up Bible verses that talk about a virtue that was mentioned in the story. On December 2nd you could look up "contentment" in a concordance and read a few passages. There are lots of different ways that you can make this experience more meaningful for your family. Just make sure that you have fun!

I've tried to include activities that will appeal to a variety of age groups. Obviously not every activity will be fun for each child. On several days I give two or more options; you can pick the one that will be enjoyed the most.

Thank you for taking the time to read this introduction and I pray that your family will grow closer to each other and to God during this Christmas season.

May the Lord bless you this Christmas season,
Amy Puetz Fox

A Merry Christmas
By Frances Ridley Havergal

"A Merry Christmas to you!"
For we serve the Lord with mirth,
And we carol forth glad tidings
Of our holy Savior's birth.
So we keep the olden greeting
With its meaning deep and true,
And with "A Merry Christmas"
And a happy New Year to you!

Oh, yes! "A Merry Christmas"
With blithest song and smile,
Bright with the thought of Him who dwelt
On earth a little while,
That we might dwell forever
Where never falls a tear:
So "A Merry Christmas" to you,
And a happy, happy year!

December 1

Becky's Christmas Dream
By Louisa May Alcott

All alone, by the kitchen fire, sat little Becky, for everyone else had gone away to keep Christmas and left her to take care of the house. Nobody had thought to give her any presents, or take her to any merrymaking, or remembered that Christmas should be made a happy time to every child, whether poor or rich. She was only twelve years old—this little girl from the poorhouse, who was bound to work for the farmer's wife till she was eighteen. She had no father or mother, no friends or home but this, and as she sat alone by the fire her little heart ached for someone to love and cherish her.

Becky was a shy, quiet child, with a thin face and wistful eyes that always seemed trying to find something that she wanted very much. She worked away, day after day, so patiently and silently that no one ever guessed what curious thoughts filled the little cropped head, or what a tender child's heart was hidden under the blue checked pinafore.

Tonight she was wishing that there were fairies in the world, who would whisk down the chimney and give her quantities of pretty things, as they did in the delightful fairy tales.

"I'm sure I am as poor and lonely as Cinderella, and need a kind godmother to help me as much as ever she did," said Becky to herself. She sat on her little stool staring at the fire, which didn't burn very well, for she felt too much out of sorts to care whether things looked cheerful or not.

There is an old belief that all dumb things can speak for one hour on Christmas Eve. Now, Becky knew nothing of this story and no one can say whether what happened was true or whether she fell asleep and dreamed it. But certain it is when Becky compared herself to Cinderella, she was amazed to hear a small voice reply,

"Well, my dear, if you want advice, I shall be very glad to give you some, for I've had much experience in this trying world."

Becky stared about her, but all she saw was the old gray cat, blinking at the fire.

"Did you speak, Tabby?" said the child, at last.

"Of course I did. If you wish a godmother, here I am."

Becky laughed at the idea; but Puss, with her silver-gray suit, white handkerchief crossed on her bosom, kind, motherly old face, and cozy purr, did make a very good Quakerish little godmother after all.

"Well, ma'am, I'm ready to listen," said Becky respectfully.

"First, my child, what do you want most?" asked the godmother, quite in the fairy-book style.

"To be loved by everybody," answered Becky.

"Good!" said the cat. "I'm pleased with that answer, it's sensible, and I'll tell you how to get your wish. Learn to make people love you by loving them."

"I don't know how," sighed Becky.

"No more did I in the beginning," returned Puss. "When I first came here, a shy young kitten, I thought only of keeping out of everybody's way, for I was afraid of everyone. I hid under the barn and only came out when no one was near. I wasn't happy, for I wanted to be petted, but didn't know how to begin.

"One day I heard Aunt Sally say to the master, 'James, that wild kitten isn't any use at all, you had better drown her and get a nice tame one to amuse the children and clear the house of mice.'

"'The poor thing has been abused, I guess, so we will give her another trial and maybe she will come to trust us after a while,' said the good master.

"I thought over these things as I lay under the barn and resolved to do my best, for I did not want to be drowned. It was hard at first, but I began by coming out when little Jane called me and letting her play with me. Then I ventured into the house, and finding a welcome at my first visit, I went again and took a mouse with me to show that I wasn't idle. No one hurt or frightened me and soon I was the household pet. For several years I have led a happy life here."

Becky listened eagerly and when Puss had ended she said timidly, "Do you think if I try not to be afraid, but to show that I want to be affectionate, the people will let me and will like it?"

"Very sure. I heard the mistress say you were a good, handy little thing. Do as I did, my dear, and you will find that there is plenty of love in the world."

"I will. Thank you, dear old Puss, for your advice."

Puss came to rub her soft cheek against Becky's hand, and then settled herself in a cozy hunch in Becky's lap. Presently another voice spoke—a queer, monotonous voice, high above her.

"Tick, tick; wish again, little Becky, and I'll tell you how to find your wish."

It was the old moon-faced clock behind the door, which had struck twelve just before Tabby first spoke.

"Dear me," said Becky, "how queerly things do act tonight!" She thought a moment then said soberly, "I wish I liked my work better. Washing dishes, picking chips and hemming towels is such tiresome work, I don't see how I can go on doing it for six more years."

"Just what I used to feel," said the clock. "I couldn't bear to think that I had to stand here and do nothing but tick year after year. I flatly said I wouldn't, and I stopped a dozen times a day. Bless me, what a fuss I made until I was put in this corner to stand idle for several months. At first I rejoiced, then I got tired of doing nothing and began to reflect that as I was born a clock, it would be wiser to do my duty and get some satisfaction out of it if I could."

"And so you went to going again—please teach me to be faithful and to love my duty," cried Becky.

"I will," and the old clock grandly struck the half hour, with a smile on its round face, as it steadily ticked on.

Here the fire blazed up and the tea-kettle hanging on the crane began to sing.

"How cheerful that is!" said Becky, as the whole kitchen brightened with the ruddy glow. "If I could have a third wish, I'd wish to be as cheerful as the fire."

"Have your wish if you choose, but you must work for it, as I do," cried the fire, as its flames embraced the old kettle till it gurgled with pleasure.

Becky thought she heard a queer voice humming these words:

*"I'm an old black kettle,
With a very crooked nose,
But I can't help being happy
When the jolly fire glows."*

"I shouldn't wonder a mite if that child had been up to mischief tonight, rummaged all over the house, eaten herself sick, or stolen something and run away with it," fretted Aunt Sally, as the family went jingling home in the big sleigh about one o'clock from the Christmas party.

"Tut, tut, Aunty, I wouldn't think evil of the poor little thing. If I'd had my way she would have gone with us and had a good time. She doesn't look as if she had seen many, and I have a notion it is what she needs," said the farmer kindly.

"The thought of her alone at home has worried me all the evening, but she didn't seem to mind, and I haven't had time to get a respectable dress ready for her to wear, so I let it go," added the farmer's wife, as she cuddled little Jane under the cloaks and shawls, with a regretful memory of Becky knocking at her heart.

"I've got some popcorn and a bouncing big apple for her," said Billy, the red-faced lad perched up by his father playing drive.

"And I'll give her one of my dolls. She said she never had one, wasn't that dreadful?" put in little Jane, popping out her head like a bird from its nest.

"Better see what she has been doing first," advised Aunt Sally. "If she hasn't done any mischief and has remembered to have the kettle boiling so I can have a cup of hot tea after my ride, and if she has kept the fire up and warmed my slippers, I don't know but I'll give her the red mittens I knitted."

They found poor Becky lying on the bare floor, her head pillowed on the stool, and old

Tabby in her arms, with a corner of the blue pinafore spread over her. The fire was burning splendidly, the kettle simmering, and in a row upon the hearth stood, not only Aunt Sally's old slippers, but those of master and mistress also, and over a chair hung two little nightgowns warming for the children.

"Well now, if that don't beat all for thoughtfulness and sense! Becky shall have them mittens, and I'll knit her a couple of pair of stockings as sure as she's living," said Aunt Sally, completely won by this unusual proof of "forehandedness" in a servant.

So Aunt Sally laid the pretty mittens close to the little rough hand that had worked so busily all day. Billy set his big red apple and bag of popcorn just where she would see them when she woke. Jane laid the doll in Becky's arms, and Tabby smelt of it approvingly, to the children's delight. The farmer had no present ready, but he stroked the little cropped head with a fatherly touch that made Becky smile in her sleep, as he said within himself, "I will do by this forlorn child as I would wish any one to do by my Janey if she were left alone." But the mother gave the best gift of all, for she stooped down and kissed Becky as only mothers can kiss. The good woman's heart reproached her for neglect of the child who had no mother.

That unusual touch wakened Becky at once, and looking about her with astonished eyes, she saw such a wonderful change in all the faces, that she clapped her hands and cried with a happy laugh, "My dream's come true! Oh, my dream's come true!"

A Christmas Carol for Children
By Martin Luther

Good news from heaven the angels bring,
Glad tidings to the earth they sing:
To us this day a child is given,
To crown us with the joy of heaven.

This is the Christ, our God and Lord,
Who in all need shall aid afford:
He will Himself our Saviour be,
From sin and sorrow set us free.

To us that blessedness He brings,
Which from the Father's bounty springs:
That in the heavenly realm we may
With Him enjoy eternal day.

All hail, Thou noble Guest, this morn,
Whose love did not the sinner scorn!
In my distress Thou cam'st to me:
What thanks shall I return to Thee?

Were earth a thousand times as fair,
Beset with gold and jewels rare,
She yet were far too poor to be
A narrow cradle, Lord, for Thee.

Ah, dearest Jesus, Holy Child!
Make Thee a bed, soft, undefiled,
Within my heart, that it may be
A quiet chamber kept for Thee.

Praise God upon His heavenly throne,
Who gave to us His only Son:
For this His hosts, on joyful wing,
A blest New Year of mercy sing.

Christmas Games

Blind-Man's Buff *by Laura Valentine*

This game was a favorite of early Victorians. Charles Dickens mentions it several times in A Christmas Carol. It is a perfect addition to our modern Christmas traditions. ~Amy

A blindfolded player is led into the center of a room, taken by the shoulders, and turned about three times, after which he must catch somebody to replace him.

Blind-man's Buff is a very ancient game; it was invented by the Greeks; the Italians call it the "Blind Cat." Gustavus, the great king of Sweden, often took pleasure in playing this game with the officers of his army.

The English name, "Hoodman-blind," is derived from the manner of blindfolding formerly in use. When caps were worn which could be drawn at will over the face, the caps, reversed so as to cover the countenance, formed the mask. This game belongs to all ages and most countries, and is known by many different names, frequently taken from animals, for example: "Blind Cow" in Germany; "Blind Goat" in Sweden; "Blind Mouse" in South Germany and Servia; "Blind Hen" in Spain. To the English name, "Blind-Man's Buff," correspond the Polish "Blind Old Man," and the Norwegian "Blind Thief."

A familiar variation makes this a ring-game. The blindfolded person stands in the center, with a staff, while the ring circles about him. When he strikes the floor three times, the ring must pause. The person in whose direction he points must grasp the staff, and utter some sound, disguising the voice as much as possible. The first must then guess the name from the sound. In New York this form of the game is called " Peggy in the Ring," and the request is "to squeak."

Hunt the Slipper *by Laura Valentine*

The game is played thus: The players (who should be many) sit in a circle close together on low stools or on the carpet. In the center of the group stands the one who is to "chase the slipper by its sound."

The players' hands are clasped behind their backs, one of them holding a slipper. The center player, of course, must not know who holds it. If there are a sufficient number of players, it adds greatly to the fun of this game to make an outer and inner circle. The slipper is passed from hand to hand; at length someone taps with it on the ground outside the circle. The hunter darts to the place indicated by the sound, but, alas! Too late generally to catch it. While seeking it there, he or she hears it tap the floor in quite an opposite direction, and again darts off on a vain search. It is generally some time before the slipper is caught. When it is, the hunter sits down, and the player from whom he or she obtained it takes his or her place.

December 2

The Fir-Tree
By Hans Christian Andersen

Out in the woods stood a nice little Fir-tree. The place he had was a very good one; the sun shone on him; as to fresh air, there was enough of that, and round him grew many large-sized comrades, pines as well as firs. But the little Fir wanted so very much to be a grown-up tree.

He did not think of the warm sun and of the fresh air; he did not care for the little cottage children that ran about and prattled when they were in the woods looking for wild strawberries. The children often came with a whole pitcher full of berries, or a long row of them threaded on a straw, and sat down near the young tree and said, "Oh, how pretty he is! What a nice little fir!" But this was what the Tree could not bear to hear.

At the end of a year he had shot up a good deal, and after another year he was another long bit taller; for with fir-trees one can always tell by the shoots how many years old they are.

"Oh, were I but such a high tree as the others are!" sighed he. "Then I should be able to spread out my branches, and with the tops to look into the wide world! Then would the birds build nests among my branches; and when there was a breeze, I could bend with as much stateliness as the others!"

Neither the sunbeams, nor the birds, nor the red clouds, which morning and evening sailed above them, gave the little Tree any pleasure.

In winter, when the snow lay glittering on the ground, a hare would often come leaping along, and jump right over the little Tree. Oh, that made him so angry! But two winters were past, and in the third the tree was so large that the hare was obliged to go round it. "To grow and grow, to get older and be tall," thought the Tree, "that, after all, is the most delightful thing in the world!"

In autumn the wood-cutters always came and felled some of the largest trees. This happened every year; and the young Fir-tree, that had now grown to a very comely size, trembled at the sight; for the magnificent great trees fell to the earth with noise and cracking, the branches were lopped off, and the trees looked long and bare; they were hardly to be recognized; and then they were laid in carts, and the horses dragged them out of the woods.

Where did they go to? What became of them?

In spring, when the Swallows and the Storks came, the Tree asked them, "Don't you know where they have been taken? Have you not met them anywhere?"

The Swallows did not know anything about it; but the Stork looked musing, nodded his head, and said: "Yes, I think I know; I met many ships as I was flying hither from Egypt; on the ships were magnificent masts, and I venture to assert that it was they that smelt so of fir. I may congratulate you, for they lifted themselves on high most majestically!"

"Oh, were I but old enough to fly across the sea! But how does the sea look in reality? What is it like?"

"That would take a long time to explain," said the Stork, and with these words off he went.

"Rejoice in thy growth!" said the Sunbeams, "Rejoice in thy vigorous growth, and in the fresh life that moveth within thee!"

And the Wind kissed the Tree, and the Dew wept tears over him; but the Fir understood it not.

When Christmas came, quite young trees were cut down; trees which often were not even as large or of the same age as this Fir-tree, who could never rest, but always wanted to be off. These young trees, and they were always the finest looking, retained their branches; they were laid on carts, and the horses drew them out of the woods.

"Where are they going to?" asked the Fir. "They are not taller than I; there was one indeed that was considerably shorter; and why do they retain all their branches? Whither are they taken?"

"We know! We know!" chirped the Sparrows. "We have peeped in at the windows in the town below! We know whither they are taken! The greatest splendor and the greatest magnificence one can imagine await them. We peeped through the windows, and saw them planted in the middle of the warm room, and ornamented with the most splendid things—with gilded apples, with gingerbread, with toys, and many hundred lights!"

"And then?" asked the Fir-tree, trembling in every bough. "And then? What happens then?"

"We did not see anything more, it was incomparably beautiful."

"I would fain know if I am destined for so glorious a career," cried the Tree, rejoicing. "That is still better than to cross the sea! What a longing do I suffer! Were Christmas but come! I am now tall, and my branches spread like the others that were carried off last year! Oh, were I but already on the cart. Were I in the warm room with all the splendor and magnificence! Yes; then something better, something still grander, will surely follow, or wherefore should they thus ornament me? Something better, something still grander, MUST follow—but what? Oh, how I long, how I suffer! I do not know myself what is the matter with me!"

"Rejoice in our presence!" said the Air and the Sunlight, "Rejoice in thy own fresh youth!"

But the Tree did not rejoice at all; he grew and grew, and was green both winter and summer. People that saw him said, "What a fine tree!" and toward Christmas he was one of the first that was cut down. The axe struck deep into the very pith; the tree fell to the earth with a sigh: he felt a pang—it was like a swoon; he could not think of happiness, for he was sorrowful at being separated from his home, from the place where he had sprung up. He knew well that he should never see his dear old comrades, the little bushes and flowers around him, any more; perhaps not even the birds! The departure was not at all agreeable.

The Tree only came to himself when he was unloaded in a courtyard with the other trees, and heard a man say, "That one is splendid! We don't want the others." Then two servants came in rich livery and carried the Fir-tree into a large and splendid drawing room. Portraits were hanging on the walls, and near the white porcelain stove stood two large Chinese vases with lions on the covers. There, too, were large easy chairs, silken sofas, large tables full of picture-books, and full of toys worth hundreds and hundreds of crowns—at least the children said so. And the Fir-tree was stuck upright in a cask that was filled with sand: but no one could see that it was a cask, for green cloth was hung all around it, and it stood on a large gaily colored carpet. Oh, how the Tree quivered! What was to happen? The servants, as well as the young ladies, decorated it. On one branch there hung little nets cut out of colored paper, and each net was filled with sugar-plums; and among the other boughs gilded apples and walnuts were suspended, looking as though they had grown there, and little blue and white tapers were placed among the leaves. Dolls that looked for all the world like men—the Tree had never beheld such before—were seen among the foliage, and at the very top a large star of gold tinsel was fixed. It was really splendid—beyond description splendid.

"This evening!" said they all; "how it will shine this evening!"

"Oh," thought the Tree, "if the evening were but come! If the tapers were but lighted! And then I wonder what will happen! Perhaps the other trees from the forest will come to look at me! Perhaps the sparrows will beat against the window-panes! I wonder if I shall take root here, and winter and summer stand covered with ornaments!"

He knew very much about the matter! But he was so impatient that for sheer longing he got a pain in his back, and this with trees is the same thing as a headache with us.

The candles were now lighted. What brightness! What splendor! The Tree trembled so in every bough that one of the tapers set fire to the foliage. It blazed up splendidly.

"Help! Help!" cried the young ladies, and they quickly put out the fire.

Now the Tree did not even dare tremble. What a state he was in! He was so uneasy lest he should lose something of his splendor, that he was quite bewildered amidst the glare and brightness; when suddenly both folding-doors opened, and a troop of children rushed in as if they would upset the Tree. The older persons followed quietly; the little ones stood quite still. But it was only for a moment; then they shouted so that the whole place reechoed with their rejoicing; they danced round the tree, and one present after the other was pulled off.

"What are they about?" thought the Tree. "What is to happen now?" And the lights burned down to the very branches, and as they burned down they were put out, one after the other, and then the children had permission to plunder the tree. So they fell upon it with such violence that all its branches cracked; if it had not been fixed firmly in the cask, it would certainly have tumbled down.

The children danced about with their beautiful playthings: no one looked at the Tree except the old nurse, who peeped between the branches; but it was only to see if there was a fig or an apple left that had been forgotten.

"A story! A story!" cried the children, drawing a little fat man toward the tree. He seated himself under it, and said: "Now we are in the shade, and the Tree can listen, too. But I shall tell only one story. Now which will you have: that about Ivedy-Avedy, or about Klumpy-Dumpy who tumbled downstairs, and yet after all came to the throne and married the princess?"

"Ivedy-Avedy!" cried some; "Klumpy-Dumpy" cried the others. There was such a bawling and screaming—the Fir-tree alone was silent, and he thought to himself, "Am I not to bawl with the rest? Am I to do nothing whatever?" For he was one of the company, and had done what he had to do.

And the man told about Klumpy-Dumpy that tumbled down, who notwithstanding came to the throne, and at last married the princess. And the children clapped their hands, and cried out, "Oh, go on! Do go on!" They wanted to hear about Ivedy-Avedy, too, but the little man only told them about Klumpy-Dumpy. The Fir-tree stood quite still and absorbed in thought; the birds in the woods had never related the like of this. "Klumpy-Dumpy fell downstairs, and yet he married the princess! Yes! Yes! That's the way of the world!" thought the Fir-tree, and believed it all, because the man who told the story was so good-looking. "Well, well! Who knows, perhaps I may fall downstairs, too, and get a princess as wife!" And he looked forward with joy to the morrow, when he hoped to be decked out again with lights, playthings, fruits, and tinsel.

"I won't tremble tomorrow," thought the Fir-tree. "I will enjoy to the full all my splendor. Tomorrow I shall hear again the story of Klumpy-Dumpy, and perhaps that of Ivedy-Avedy, too." And the whole night the Tree stood still and in deep thought.

In the morning the servant and the housemaid came in.

"Now, then, the splendor will begin again," thought the Fir. But they dragged him out of the room, and up the stairs into the loft; and here in a dark corner, where no daylight could enter, they left him. "What's the meaning of this?" thought the Tree. "What am I to do here? What shall I hear now, I wonder?" And he leaned against the wall, lost in reverie. Time enough had he, too, for his reflections; for days and nights passed on, and nobody came up; and when at last somebody did come, it was only to put some great trunks in a corner out of the way. There stood the Tree quite hidden; it seemed as if he had been entirely forgotten.

"'Tis now winter out of doors!" thought the Tree. "The earth is hard and covered with snow; men cannot plant me now, and therefore I have been put up here under shelter till the springtime comes! How thoughtful that is! How kind man is, after all! If it only were not so dark here, and so terribly lonely! Not even a hare. And out in the woods it was so pleasant, when the snow was on the ground, and the hare leaped by; yes—even when he jumped over me; but I did not like it then. It is really terribly lonely here!"

"Squeak! Squeak!" said a little Mouse at the same moment, peeping out of his hole. And then another little one came. They sniffed about the Fir-tree, and rustled among the branches.

"It is dreadfully cold," said the Mouse. "But for that, it would be delightful here, old Fir, wouldn't it?"

"I am by no means old," said the Fir-tree. "There's many a one considerably older than I am."

"Where do you come from," asked the Mice, "and what can you do?" They were so extremely curious. "Tell us about the most beautiful spot on the earth. Have you never been there? Were you never in the larder, where cheeses lie on the shelves, and hams hang from above; where one dances about on tallow candles; that place where one enters lean, and comes out again fat and portly?"

"I know no such place," said the Tree, "but I know the woods, where the sun shines, and where the little birds sing." And then he told all about his youth; and the little Mice had never heard the like before; and they listened and said:

"Well, to be sure! How much you have seen! How happy you must have been!"

"I?" said the Fir-tree, thinking over what he had himself related. "Yes, in reality those were happy times." And then he told about Christmas Eve, when he was decked out with cakes and candles.

"Oh," said the little Mice, "how fortunate you have been, old Fir-tree!"

"I am by no means old," said he. "I came from the woods this winter; I am in my prime, and am only rather short for my age."

"What delightful stories you know!" said the Mice and the next night they came with four other little Mice, who were to hear what the tree recounted; and the more he related, the more plainly he remembered all himself; and it appeared as if those times had really been happy times. "But they may still come—they may still come. Klumpy-Dumpy fell downstairs and yet he got a princess," and he thought at the moment of a nice little Birch-tree growing out in the woods; to the Fir, that would be a real charming princess.

"Who is Klumpy-Dumpy?" asked the Mice. So then the Fir-tree told the whole fairy tale, for he could remember every single word of it; and the little Mice jumped for joy up to the very top of the Tree. Next night two more Mice came, and on Sunday two Rats, even; but they said the stories were not interesting, which vexed the little Mice; and they, too, now began to think them not so very amusing either.

"Do you know only one story?" asked the Rats.

"Only that one," answered the Tree. "I heard it on my happiest evening; but I did not then know how happy I was."

"It is a very stupid story. Don't you know one about bacon and tallow candles? Can't you tell any larder stories?"

"No," said the Tree.

"Then good-bye," said the Rats; and they went home.

At last the little Mice stayed away also; and the Tree sighed: "After all, it was very pleasant when the sleek little Mice sat around me and listened to what I told them. Now that too is over. But I will take good care to enjoy myself when I am brought out again."

But when was that to be? Why, one morning there came a quantity of people who set to work in the loft. The trunks were moved, the Tree was pulled out and thrown—rather hard, it is true—down on the floor, but a man drew him toward the stairs, where the daylight shone.

"Now a merry life will begin again," thought the Tree. He felt the fresh air, the first sunbeam, and now he was out in the courtyard. All passed so quickly, there was so much going on around him, that the Tree quite forgot to look to himself. The court adjoined a garden, and all was in flower; the roses hung so fresh and odorous over the balustrade, the lindens were in blossom, the Swallows flew by, and said, "Quirre-vit! My husband is come!" But it was not the Fir-tree that they meant.

"Now, then, I shall really enjoy life," said he, exultingly, and spread out his branches; but, alas! They were all withered and yellow. It was in a corner that he lay, among weeds and nettles. The golden star of tinsel was still on the top of the Tree, and glittered in the sunshine.

In the courtyard some of the merry children were playing who had danced at Christmas round the Fir-tree, and were so glad at the sight of him. One of the youngest ran and tore off the golden star.

"Only look what is still on the ugly old Christmas tree!" said he, trampling on the branches, so that they all cracked beneath his feet. And the Tree beheld all the beauty of the flowers, and the freshness in the garden; he beheld himself, and wished he had remained in his dark corner in the loft; he thought of his first youth in the woods, of the merry Christmas Eve, and of the little Mice who had listened with so much pleasure to the story of Klumpy-Dumpy.

"'Tis over—'tis past!" said the poor Tree. "Had I but rejoiced when I had reason to do so! But now 'tis past, 'tis past!"

And the gardener's boy chopped the Tree into small pieces; there was a whole heap lying there. The wood flamed up splendidly under the large brewing copper, and it sighed so deeply! Each sigh was like a shot.

The boys played about in the court, and the youngest wore the gold star on his breast which the Tree had had on the happiest evening of his life. However, that was over now—the Tree gone, the story at an end. All, all was over; every tale must end at last.

The Spirit of Christmas

From *Pickwick Papers*
By Charles Dickens

And numerous indeed are the hearts to which Christmas brings a brief season of happiness and enjoyment. How many families whose members have been dispersed and scattered far and wide, in the restless struggles of life, are then reunited, and meet once again in that happy state of companionship and mutual good-will, which is a source of such pure and unalloyed delight, and one so incompatible with the cares and sorrows of the world, that the religious belief of the most civilized nations, and the rude traditions of the roughest savages, alike number it among the first joys of a future state of existence, provided for the blest and happy! How many old recollections, and how many dormant sympathies, does Christmas time awaken!

We write these words now, many miles distant from the spot at which, year after year, we met on that day, a merry and joyous circle. Many of the hearts that throb so gaily then, have ceased to beat; many of the looks that shone so brightly then, have ceased to glow; the hands we grasped, have grown cold; the eyes we sought, have hid their luster in the grave; and yet the old house, the room, the merry voices and smiling faces, the jest, the laugh, the most minute and trivial circumstance connected with those happy meetings, crowd upon our mind at each recurrence of the season, as if the last assemblage had been but yesterday.

Happy, happy Christmas, that can win us back to the delusions of our childish days, that can recall to the old man the pleasures of his youth, and transport the sailor and the traveler, thousands of miles away, back to his own fireside and his quiet home!

Christmas Craft

Little Box Ornaments by Amy Puetz Fox

These charming ornaments have been a favorite craft in my family for years. They are very simple to make and perfect for all age groups. They make charming gifts or will make a nice addition to your own tree!
~Amy

To make them you will need: Decorative string or ribbon
Old Christmas cards   Ruler
Scissors   Pen or pencil

1. Cut a 5¼" square from an old Christmas card. Use a ruler to draw an X from each corner to the opposite one (Fig. 1).

2. Fold one corner to the center of the X and then fold again (Fig. 2). Unfold that corner and fold the three remaining corners in the same way.

3. Unfold the card. Make four cuts with scissors along four of the folds (Fig. 3).

4. Now fold corners B and D into the X (Fig. 4). The extra edges need to be pushed to the inside. See Fig. 4.

5. Fold the other two corners A and C into the center. You now have a box (Fig. 5)!

This is the top of the box. Complete these steps again for the bottom and for the two remaining boxes (see page 15 for the size of square needed for the remaining box tops and bottoms). After the three boxes are complete, stack them on top of each other and tie together with a decorative string or some decorating ribbon. Make the ribbon long enough to add a loop at the top to hang from the tree. You could cover them with wrapping paper or leave them with just the card showing.

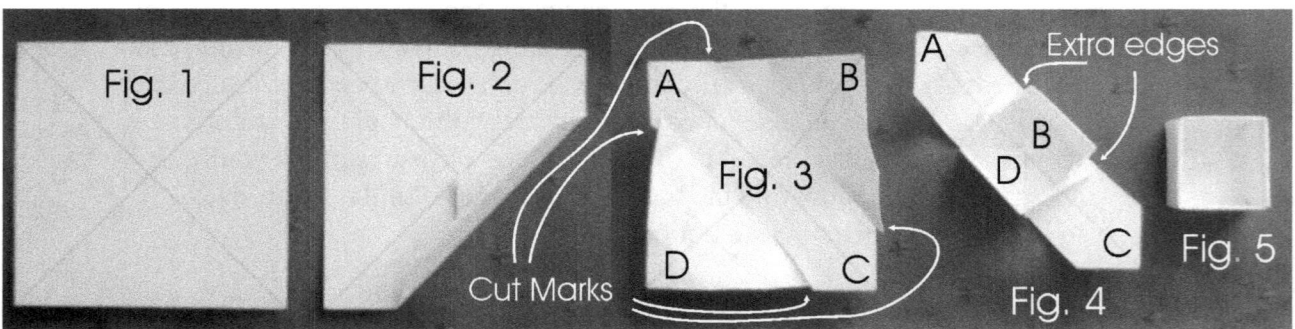

Box Sizes

Large box top 5¼ inches
Large box bottom 5 inches
Medium box top 3½ inches
Medium box bottom 3¼ inches
Small box top 2½ inches
Small box bottom 2¼ inches

To make this craft go faster, make templates out of cardstock for each box. Then you can keep them with your old cards year after year.

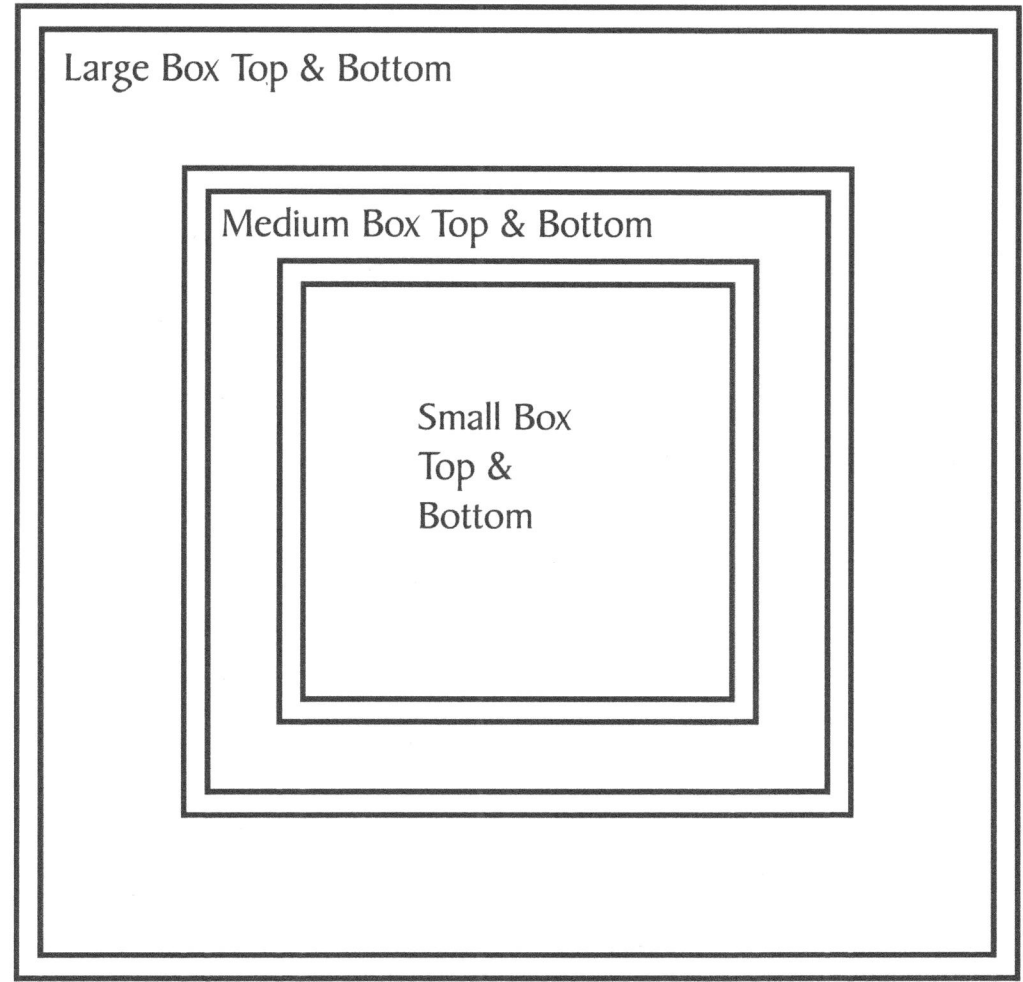

December 3

The Star
By Florence M. Kingsley

Once upon a time in a country far away from here, there lived a little girl named Ruth. Ruth's home was not at all like our houses, for she lived in a little tower on top of the great stone wall that surrounded the town of Bethlehem. Ruth's father was the hotel-keeper—the Bible says the "inn keeper." This inn was not at all like our hotels, either. There was a great open yard, which was called the courtyard. All about this yard were little rooms and each traveler who came to the hotel rented one. The inn stood near the great stone wall of the city, so that as Ruth stood, one night, looking out of the tower window, she looked directly into the courtyard. It was truly a strange sight that met her eyes. So many people were coming to the inn, for the King had made a law that every man should come back to the city where his father used to live to be counted and to pay his taxes. Some of the people came on the backs of camels, with great rolls of bedding and their dishes for cooking upon the back of the beast. Some of them came on little donkeys, and on their backs too were the bedding and the dishes. Some of the people came walking—slowly; they were so tired. Many miles some of them had come. As Ruth looked down into the courtyard, she saw the camels being led to their places by their masters, she heard the snap of the whips, she saw the sparks shoot up from the fires that were kindled in the courtyard, where each person was preparing his own supper; she heard the cries of the tired, hungry little children.

Presently her mother, who was cooking supper, came over to the window and said, "Ruthie, thou shalt hide in the house until all those people are gone. Dost thou understand?"

"Yes, my mother," said the child, and she left the window to follow her mother back to the stove, limping painfully, for little Ruth was a cripple. Her mother stooped suddenly and caught the child in her arms.

"My poor little lamb. It was a mule's kick, just six years ago, that hurt your poor back and made you lame."

"Never mind, Mother. My back does not ache today, and lately when the light of the strange new star has shone down upon my bed my back has felt so much stronger and I have felt so happy, as though I could climb upon the rays of the star and up, up into the sky and above the stars!"

Her mother shook her head sadly. "Thou art not likely to climb much, now or ever, but come, the supper is ready; let us go to find your father. I wonder what keeps him."

They found the father standing at the gate of the courtyard, talking to a man and woman who had just arrived. The man was tall, with a long beard, and he led by a rope a snow white mule, on which sat the drooping figure of the woman. As Ruth and her mother came near, they heard the father say, "But I tell thee that there is no more room in the inn. Hast thou no friends where thou canst go to spend the night?"

The man shook his head. "No, none," he answered. "I care not for myself, but my poor wife."

Little Ruth pulled at her mother's dress. "Mother, the oxen sleep out under the stars these warm nights and the straw in the caves is clean and warm; I have made a bed there for my little lamb."

Ruth's mother bowed before the tall man. "Thou didst hear the child. It is as she says—the straw is clean and warm."

The tall man bowed his head. "We shall be very glad to stay," and he helped the sweet-faced woman down from the donkey's back and led her away to the cave stable, while little Ruth and her mother hurried up the stairs that they might send a bowl of porridge to the sweet-faced woman, and a cup of new milk, as well.

* * * * *

That night when little Ruth lay down in her bed, the rays of the beautiful new star shone through the window more brightly than before. They seemed to soothe the tired aching shoulders. She fell asleep and dreamed that the beautiful, bright star burst and out of it came countless angels, who sang in the night:

"Glory to God in the highest, peace on earth, good will to men." And then it was morning and her mother was bending over her and saying, "Awake, awake, little Ruth. Mother has something to tell thee." Then as the eyes opened slowly—"The angels came in the night, little one, and left a Baby to lay beside your little white lamb in the manger."

* * * * *

That afternoon, Ruth went with her mother to the fountain. The mother turned aside to talk to the other women of the town about the strange things heard and seen the night before, but Ruth went on and sat down by the edge of the fountain. The child was not frightened, for strangers came often to the well, but never had she seen men who looked like the three who now came towards her. The first one, a tall man with a long white beard, came close to Ruth and said, "Canst tell us, child, where is born he that is called the King of the Jews?"

"I know of no king," she answered, "but last night while the star was shining, the angels brought a baby to lie beside my white lamb in the manger."

The stranger bowed his head. "That must be he. Wilt thou show us the way to Him, my child?" So Ruth ran and her mother led the three men to the cave and "when they saw the Child, they rejoiced with exceeding great joy, and opening their gifts, they presented unto Him gold, and frankincense and myrrh," with wonderful jewels, so that Ruth's mother's eyes shone with wonder, but little Ruth saw only the Baby, which lay asleep on its mother's breast.

"If only I might hold Him in my arms," she thought, but was afraid to ask.

* * * * *

After a few days, the strangers left Bethlehem, all but the three—the man, whose name was Joseph, and Mary, his wife, and the Baby. Then, as of old, little Ruth played about the courtyard and the white lamb frolicked at her side. Often she dropped to her knees to press the little woolly white head against her breast, while she murmured: "My little lamb, my very, very own. I love you, lambie," and then together they would steal over to the entrance of the cave to peep in at the Baby, and always she thought, "If I only might touch his hand," but was afraid to ask. One night as she lay in her bed, she thought to herself: "Oh, I wish I had a beautiful gift for him, such as the wise men brought, but I have nothing at all to offer and I love him so much." Just then the light of the star, which was nightly fading, fell across the foot of the bed and shone full upon the white lamb which lay asleep at her feet—and then she thought of something. The next morning she arose with her face shining with joy. She dressed carefully and with the white lamb held close to her breast, went slowly and painfully down the stairway and over to the door of the cave. "I have come," she said, "to worship Him, and I have brought Him—my white lamb." The mother smiled at the lame child, then she lifted the Baby from her breast and placed Him in the arms of the little maid who knelt at her feet.

* * * * *

A few days after, an angel came to the father, Joseph, and told him to take the Baby and hurry to the land of Egypt, for the wicked King wanted to do it harm, and so these three—the father, mother and Baby—went by night to the far country of Egypt. And the star grew dimmer and dimmer and passed away forever from the skies over Bethlehem, but little Ruth grew straight and strong and beautiful as the almond trees in the orchard, and all the people who saw her were amazed, for Ruth was once a cripple.

"It was the light of the strange star," her mother said, but little Ruth knew it was the touch of the blessed Christ-Child, who was once folded against her heart.

Christmas Quiz

In Other Words by Amy Puetz Fox

Match the definition on the left with the correct word on the right.
Answers are below.

1) Ball of gas

2) Food for cows and other barn animals

3) Songs we sing at Christmas

4) A box used to feed animals hay

5) One who looks after cud-chewing animals of the wooly kind

6) The manager of a lodging establishment

7) Those who came from the east

8) A messenger of God

9) Incense of gum resin from Arabian trees

10) A precious metal

11) It is used to make perfume

12) A place where animals live

13) A fee paid to the king

14) The head of the whole Roman world

15) The Caesar who ruled when Jesus was born

16) The angel who appeared to Zechariah, Mary, and Joseph

A) Angel

B) Magi

C) Carols

D) Frankincense

E) Stable

F) Shepherd

G) Manger

H) Augustus

I) Hay

J) Caesar

K) Star

L) Tax

M) Gabriel

N) Myrrh

O) Gold

P) Inn Keeper

Answers
1-K, 2-I, 3-C, 4-G, 5-F, 6-P, 7-B, 8-A, 9-D, 10-O, 11-N, 12-E, 13-L, 14-J, 15-H, 16-M

December 4

The Conscience-Pudding
Part 1
By E. Nesbit
From New Treasure Seekers Chapter 2

It was Christmas, nearly a year after Mother died. I cannot write about Mother—but I will just say one thing. If she had only been away for a little while, and not for always, we shouldn't have been so keen on having a Christmas. I didn't understand this then, but I am much older now, and I think it was just because everything was so different and horrid we felt we must do something; and perhaps we were not particular enough what. Things make you much more unhappy when you loaf about than when you are doing events.

Father had to go away just about Christmas. He had heard that his wicked partner, who ran away with his money, was in France, and he thought he could catch him, but really he was in Spain, where catching criminals is never practiced. We did not know this till afterwards.

Before Father went away he took Dora and Oswald into his study, and said—

"I'm awfully sorry I've got to go away, but it is very serious business, and I must go. You'll be good while I'm away, kiddies, won't you?"

We promised faithfully. Then he said—

"There are reasons—you wouldn't understand if I tried to tell you but you can't have much of a Christmas this year. But I've told Matilda to make you a good plain pudding. Perhaps next Christmas will be brighter." (It was; for the next Christmas saw us the affluent nephews and nieces of an Indian uncle—but that is quite another story, as good old Kipling says.)

When Father had been seen off at Lewisham Station with his bags, and a plaid rug in a strap, we came home again, and it was horrid. There were papers and things littered all over his room where he had packed. We tidied the room up—it was the only thing we could do for him. It was Dicky who accidentally broke his shaving-glass, and H.O. made a paper boat out of a letter we found out afterwards Father particularly wanted to keep. This took us some time, and when we went into the nursery the fire was black out, and we could not get it alight again, even with the whole Daily Chronicle. Matilda, who was our general then, was out, as well as the fire, so we went and sat in the kitchen. There is always a good fire in kitchens. The kitchen hearthrug was not nice to sit on, so we spread newspapers on it.

It was sitting in the kitchen, I think, that brought to our minds my Father's parting words—about the pudding, I mean.

Oswald said, "Father said we couldn't have much of a Christmas for secret reasons, and he said he had told Matilda to make us a plain pudding."

The plain pudding instantly cast its shadow over the deepening gloom of our young minds.

"I wonder how plain she'll make it?" Dicky said.

"As plain as plain, you may depend," said Oswald. "A here-am-I-where-are-you pudding—that's her sort."

The others groaned, and we gathered closer round the fire till the newspapers rustled madly.

"I believe I could make a pudding that wasn't plain, if I tried," Alice said. "Why shouldn't we?"

"No chink," said Oswald, with brief sadness.

"How much would it cost?" Noël asked, and added that Dora had twopence and H.O. had a French halfpenny.

Dora got the cookery-book out of the dresser drawer, where it lay doubled up among clothes-pegs, dirty dusters, scallop shells, string, penny novelettes, and the dining-room corkscrew. The general we had then—it seemed as if she did all the cooking on the cookery-book instead of on the baking-board, there were traces of so many bygone meals upon its pages.

"It doesn't say Christmas pudding at all," said Dora.

"Try plum," the resourceful Oswald instantly counseled.

Dora turned the greasy pages anxiously.

"Plum-pudding, 518."

"A rich, with flour, 517."

"Christmas, 517."

"Good without eggs, 518."

"Plain, 518."

"We don't want that anyhow. 'Christmas, 517'—that's the one."

It took her a long time to find the page. Oswald got a shovel of coals and made up the fire. It blazed up like the devouring elephant the Daily Telegraph always calls it. Then Dora read—

"Christmas plum-pudding. Time six hours."

"To eat it in?" said H.O.

"No, silly! To make it."

"Forge ahead, Dora," Dicky replied.

Dora went on, "One pound and a half of raisins; half a pound of currants; three quarters of a pound of breadcrumbs; half a pound of flour; three-quarters of a pound of beef suet; nine eggs; one wine glassful of brandy; half a pound of citron and orange peel; half a nutmeg; and a little ground ginger. I wonder how little ground ginger?"

"A teacupful would be enough, I think," Alice said; "we must not be extravagant."

"We haven't got anything yet to be extravagant with," said Oswald, who had a toothache that day. "What would you do with the things if you'd got them?"

"You'd 'chop the suet as fine as possible'—I wonder how fine that is?" replied Dora and the book together—"and mix it with the breadcrumbs and flour; add the currants washed and dried."

"Not starched, then," said Alice.

"'The citron and orange peel cut into thin slices'—I wonder what they call thin? Matilda's thin bread-and-butter is quite different from what I mean by it—'and the raisins stoned and divided.' How many heaps would you divide them into?"

"Seven, I suppose," said Alice; "one for each person and one for the pot—I mean pudding."

"'Mix it all well together with the grated nutmeg and ginger. Then stir in nine eggs well beaten, and the brandy'—we'll leave that out, I think—'and again mix it thoroughly together that every ingredient may be moistened; put it into a buttered mould, tie over tightly, and boil for six hours. Serve it ornamented with holly and brandy poured over it.'"

"I should think holly and brandy poured over it would be simply beastly," said Dicky.

"I expect the book knows. I daresay holly and water would do as well though. 'This pudding may be made a month before'—it's no use reading about that though, because we've only got four days to Christmas."

"It's no use reading about any of it," said Oswald, with thoughtful repeatedness, "because we haven't got the things, and we haven't got the coin to get them."

"We might get the tin somehow," said Dicky.

"There must be lots of kind people who would subscribe to a Christmas pudding for poor children who hadn't any," Noël said.

"Well, I'm going skating at Penn's," said Oswald. "It's no use thinking about puddings. We must put up with it plain."

So he went, and Dicky went with him.

When they returned to their home in the evening the fire had been lighted again in the nursery, and the others were just having tea. We toasted our bread-and-butter on the bare side, and it gets a little warm among the butter. This is called French toast. "I like English better, but it is more expensive," Alice said—

"Matilda is in a frightful rage about your putting those coals on the kitchen fire, Oswald. She says we shan't have enough to last over Christmas as it is. And Father gave her a talking to before he went about them—asked her if she ate them, she says—but I don't believe he did. Anyway, she's locked the coal-cellar door, and she's got the key in her pocket. I don't see how we can boil the pudding."

"What pudding?" said Oswald dreamily. He was thinking of a chap he had seen at Penn's who had cut the date 1899 on the ice with four strokes.

"The pudding," Alice said. "Oh, we've had such a time, Oswald! First Dora and I went to the shops to find out exactly what the pudding would cost—it's only two and elevenpence halfpenny, counting in the holly."

"It's no good," Oswald repeated; he is very patient and will say the same thing any number of times. "It's no good. You know we've got no tin."

"Ah," said Alice, "but Noël and I went out, and we called at some of the houses in Granville

Park and Dartmouth Hill—and we got a lot of sixpences and shillings, besides pennies, and one old gentleman gave us half-a-crown. He was so nice. Quite bald, with a knitted red and blue waistcoat. We've got eight-and-sevenpence."

Oswald did not feel quite sure Father would like us to go asking for shillings and sixpences, or even half-crowns from strangers, but he did not say so. The money had been asked for and got, and it couldn't be helped—and perhaps he wanted the pudding—I am not able to remember exactly why he did not speak up and say, "This is wrong," but anyway he didn't.

Alice and Dora went out and bought the things next morning. They bought double quantities, so that it came to five shillings and elevenpence, and was enough to make a noble pudding. There was a lot of holly left over for decorations. We used very little for the sauce. The money that was left we spent very anxiously in other things to eat, such as dates and figs and toffee.

We did not tell Matilda about it. She was a red-haired girl, and apt to turn shirty at the least thing.

Concealed under our jackets and overcoats we carried the parcels up to the nursery, and hid them in the treasure-chest we had there. It was the bureau drawer. It was locked up afterwards because the treacle got all over the green baize and the little drawers inside it while we were waiting to begin to make the pudding. It was the grocer told us we ought to put treacle in the pudding, and also about not so much ginger as a teacupful.

When Matilda had begun to pretend to scrub the floor (she pretended this three times a week so as to have an excuse not to let us in the kitchen, but I know she used to read novelettes most of the time, because Alice and I had a squint through the window more than once), we barricaded the nursery door and set to work. We were very careful to be quite clean. We washed our hands as well as the currants. I have sometimes thought we did not get all the soap off the currants. The pudding smelt like a washing-day when the time came to cut it open. And we washed a corner of the table to chop the suet on. Chopping suet looks easy till you try.

Father's machine he weighs letters with did to weigh out the things. We did this very carefully, in case the grocer had not done so. Everything was right except the raisins. H.O. had carried them home. He was very young then, and there was a hole in the corner of the paper bag and his mouth was sticky. Lots of people have been hanged to a gibbet in chains on evidence no worse than that, and we told H.O. so till he cried. This was good for him. It was not unkindness to H.O., but part of our duty. Chopping suet as fine as possible is much harder than anyone would think, as I said before. So is crumbling bread—especially if your loaf is new, like ours was. When we had done them the breadcrumbs and the suet were both very large and lumpy, and of a dingy gray color, something like pale slate pencil.

They looked a better color when we had mixed them with the flour. The girls had washed the currants with Brown Windsor soap and the sponge. Some of the currants got inside the sponge and kept coming out in the bath for days afterwards. I see now that this was not quite nice. We cut the candied peel as thin as we wish people would cut our bread-and-butter. We tried to take the stones out of the raisins, but they were too sticky, so we just divided them up in seven lots. Then we mixed the other things in the wash-hand basin from the spare bedroom that was always spare. We each put in our own lot of raisins and turned it all into a pudding-basin, and tied it up in one of Alice's pinafores, which was the nearest thing to a proper pudding-cloth we could find—at any rate clean. What was left sticking to the wash-hand basin did not taste so bad.

"It's a little bit soapy," Alice said, "but perhaps that will boil out; like stains in tablecloths."

It was a difficult question how to boil the pudding. Matilda proved furious when asked to let us, just because someone had happened to knock her hat off the scullery door and Pincher had got it and done for it. However, part of the embassy nicked a saucepan while the others were being told what Matilda thought about the hat, and we got hot water out of the bathroom and made it boil over our nursery fire. We put the pudding in—it was now getting on towards the hour of tea—and let it boil. With some exceptions—owing to the fire going down, and Matilda not hurrying up with coals—it boiled for an hour and a quarter. Then Matilda came suddenly in and said, "I'm not going to have you messing about in here with my saucepans;" and she tried to take it off the fire. You will see that we couldn't stand this; it was not likely. I do not remember who it was that told her to mind her own business, and I think I have forgotten who caught hold of her first to make her chuck it. I am sure no needless violence was used. Anyway, while the struggle progressed, Alice and Dora took the saucepan away and put it in the boot-cupboard under the stairs and put the key in their pocket.

This sharp encounter made everyone very hot and cross. We got over it before Matilda did, but we brought her round before bedtime. Quarrels should always be made up before bedtime. It says so in the Bible. If this simple rule was followed there would not be so many wars and martyrs and law suits and inquisitions and bloody deaths at the stake.

All the house was still. The gas was out all over the house except on the first landing, when several darkly-shrouded figures might have been observed creeping downstairs to the kitchen.

On the way, with superior precaution, we got out our saucepan. The kitchen fire was red, but low; the coal-cellar was locked, and there was nothing in the scuttle but a little coal-dust and the piece of brown paper that is put in to keep the coals from tumbling out through the bottom where the hole is. We put the saucepan on the fire and plied it with fuel—two Chronicles, a Telegraph, and two Family Herald novelettes were burned in vain. I am almost sure the pudding did not boil at all that night.

"Never mind," Alice said. "We can each nick a piece of coal every time we go into the kitchen tomorrow."

This daring scheme was faithfully performed, and by night we had nearly half a waste-paper basket of coal, coke, and cinders. And in the depth of night once more we might have been observed, this time with our collier-like waste-paper basket in our guarded hands.

There was more fire left in the grate that night, and we fed it with the fuel we had collected. This time the fire blazed up, and the pudding boiled like mad. This was the time it boiled two hours—at least I think it was about that, but we dropped asleep on the kitchen tables and dresser. You dare not be lowly in the night in the kitchen, because of the beetles. We were aroused by a horrible smell. It was the pudding-cloth burning. All the water had secretly boiled itself away. We filled it up at once with cold, and the saucepan cracked. So we cleaned it and put it back on the shelf and took another and went to bed. You see what a lot of trouble we had over the pudding. Every evening till Christmas, which had now become only the day after tomorrow, we sneaked down in the inky midnight and boiled that pudding for as long as it would.

To be continued . . .

Christmas Cooking

Bread Pudding

The plum pudding of this story is very different from the pudding we know today. Our puddings are a creamy dessert whereas the puddings in the story are bread puddings. Below are recipes for the two bread puddings mentioned in the story. After reading the recipes, if you really want some modern pudding, a recipe is provided for that also! ~Amy

Plain Bread Pudding by Maria Willett Howard

2 cups bread crumbs
4 cups milk
3 eggs
¼ teaspoon nutmeg
½ cup sugar
1 teaspoon salt
2 tablespoons butter

Soak bread in milk five minutes; add beaten eggs and remaining ingredients. Put into a greased 9" x 9" pan. Bake one hour at 350° or till knife inserted comes out clean. Serve with hard sauce.

Hard Sauce by Maria Willett Howard

½ cup butter
1 teaspoon hot water
1 cup powdered sugar
1 teaspoon vanilla

Cream butter; add sugar by the teaspoon, and beat until light and creamy. Flavor and serve.

Plum Pudding by Carlotta Cherryholmes Greer

2 cups soft bread crumbs
½ teaspoon baking soda
1/8 teaspoon cloves
½ teaspoon cinnamon
¼ teaspoon salt
½ cup raisins
½ cup suet
½ cup molasses
1 egg
¾ cup milk
½ cup currants

To prevent suet from sticking while being chopped, sprinkle it with a little flour. Use a meat grinder, or a chopping bowl and knife, to chop the suet. Beat the eggs lightly and add the milk to them. The currants and raisins should be sprinkled with flour. Mix the ingredients in the order given. Steam in a buttered pudding mold for at least 2 hours. Serve with caramel sauce.

Note: This recipe is from a 1915 cookbook. Shortening may be used in the place of the suet. Bake at 350° for 1 and a half to two hours. When a knife inserted in the center comes out clean it is done.

Caramel Sauce by Maria Willett Howard

1 cup sugar
1 cup boiling water

Put sugar in a sauce pan over medium heat. Stir continually until sugar is a light brown color. Add water, and simmer fifteen minutes. Serve warm.

Vanilla Pudding *by Amy Puetz Fox*

¾ cup sugar
¼ teaspoon salt
2 tablespoons cornstarch
1 egg
2 cups milk
1 teaspoon vanilla
1 tablespoon butter

In saucepan blend sugar, cornstarch, and salt. Add milk and well-beaten egg. Stir and cook over medium heat until thick and bubbling. Cook and stir four minutes more. Remove from heat, add butter and vanilla. Chill and serve.

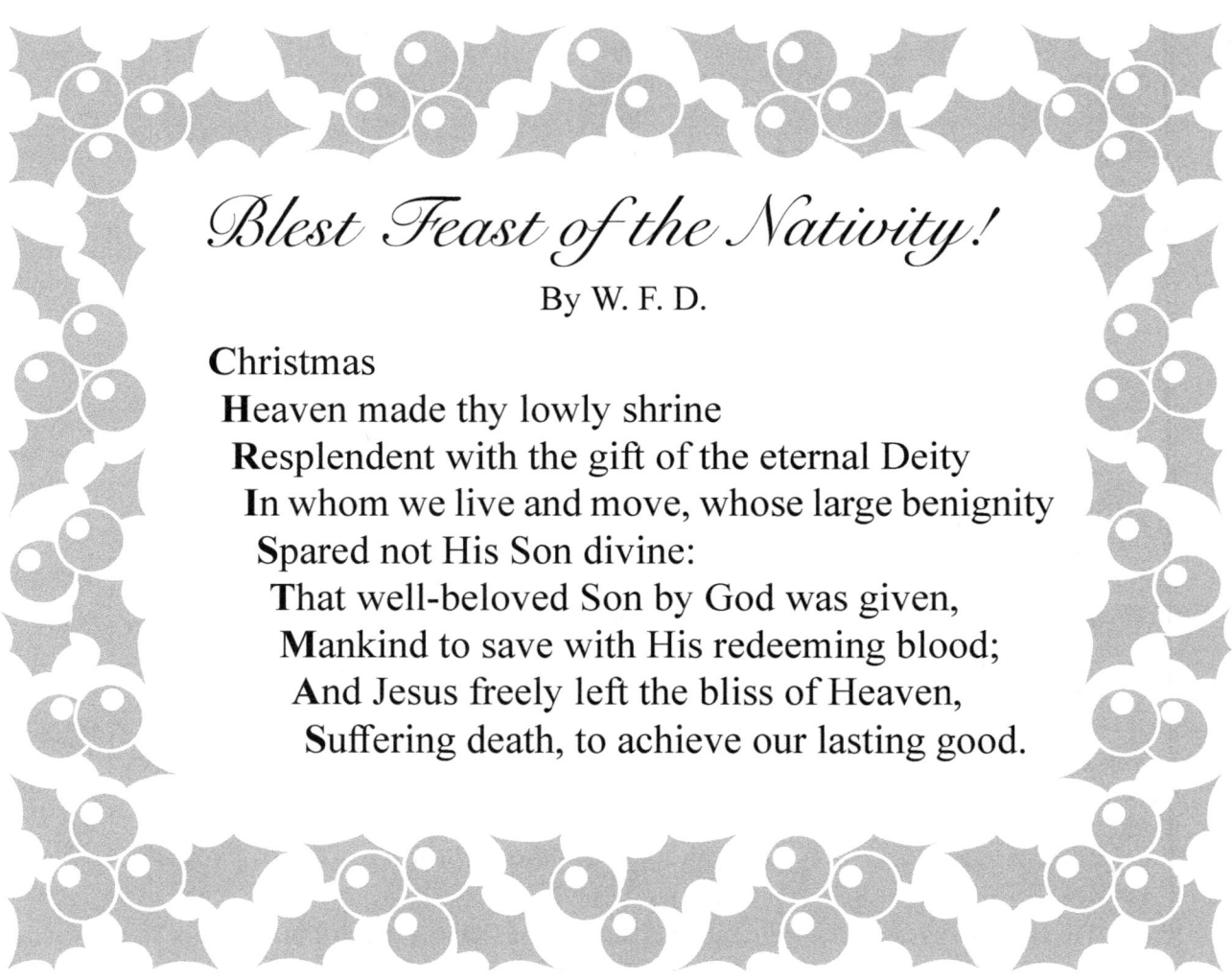

Blest Feast of the Nativity!
By W. F. D.

Christmas
 Heaven made thy lowly shrine
  Resplendent with the gift of the eternal Deity
   In whom we live and move, whose large benignity
    Spared not His Son divine:
     That well-beloved Son by God was given,
      Mankind to save with His redeeming blood;
       And Jesus freely left the bliss of Heaven,
        Suffering death, to achieve our lasting good.

December 5

The Conscience-Pudding
Part 2
By E. Nesbit
From New Treasure Seekers Chapter 2

On Christmas morning we chopped the holly for the sauce, but we put hot water (instead of brandy) and moist sugar. Some of them said it was not so bad. Oswald was not one of these.

Then came the moment when the plain pudding Father had ordered smoked upon the board. Matilda brought it in and went away at once. She had a cousin out of Woolwich Arsenal to see her that day, I remember. Those far-off days are quite distinct in memory's recollection still.

Then we got out our own pudding from its hiding-place and gave it one last hurried boil—only seven minutes, because of the general impatience which Oswald and Dora could not cope with.

We had found means to secrete a dish, and we now tried to dish the pudding up, but it stuck to the basin, and had to be dislodged with the chisel. The pudding was horribly pale. We poured the holly sauce over it, and Dora took up the knife and was just cutting it when a few simple words from H.O. turned us from happy and triumphing cookery artists to persons in despair.

He said: "How pleased all those kind ladies and gentlemen would be if they knew we were the poor children they gave the shillings and sixpences and things for!"

We all said, "What?" It was no moment for politeness.

"I say," H.O. said, "they'd be glad if they knew it was us was enjoying the pudding, and not dirty little, really poor children."

"You should say 'you were,' not 'you was,'" said Dora, but it was as in a dream and only from habit.

"Do you mean to say"—Oswald spoke firmly, yet not angrily—"that you and Alice went and begged for money for poor children, and then kept it?"

"We didn't keep it," said H.O., "we spent it."

"We've kept the things, you little duffer!" said Dicky, looking at the pudding sitting alone and uncared for on its dish. "You begged for money for poor children, and then kept it. It's stealing, that's what it is. I don't say so much about you—you're only a silly kid—but Alice knew better. Why did you do it?"

He turned to Alice, but she was now too deep in tears to get a word out. H.O. looked a bit frightened, but he answered the question. We have taught him this. He said-

"I thought they'd give us more if I said poor children than if I said just us."

"That's cheating," said Dicky "downright beastly, mean, low cheating."

"I'm not," said H.O.; "and you're another." Then he began to cry too. I do not know how the others felt, but I understand from Oswald that he felt now the honor of the house of Bastable had been stamped on in the dust, and it didn't matter what happened. He looked at the beastly holly that had been left over from the sauce and was stuck up over the pictures. It now appeared hollow and disgusting, though it had got quite a lot of berries, and some of it was the varied kind green and white. The figs and dates and toffee were set out in the doll's dinner service. The very sight of it all made Oswald blush sickly. He owns he would have liked to cuff H.O., and, if he did for a moment wish to shake Alice, the author, for one, can make allowances.

Now Alice choked and spluttered, and wiped her eyes fiercely, and said, "It's no use ragging H.O. It's my fault. I'm older than he is."

H.O. said, "It couldn't be Alice's fault. I don't see as it was wrong."

"That, not as," murmured Dora, putting her arm round the sinner who had brought this degrading blight upon our family tree, but such is girls' undetermined and affectionate silliness. "Tell sister all about it, H.O. dear. Why couldn't it be Alice's fault?"

H.O. cuddled up to Dora and said snufflingly in his nose—

"Because she hadn't got nothing to do with it. I collected it all. She never went into one of the houses. She didn't want to."

"And then took all the credit of getting the money," said Dicky savagely.

Oswald said, "Not much credit," in scornful tones.

"Oh, you are beastly, the whole lot of you, except Dora!" Alice said, stamping her foot in rage and despair. "I tore my frock on a nail going out, and I didn't want to go back, and I got H.O. to go to the houses alone, and I waited for him outside. And I asked him not to say anything because I didn't want Dora to know about the frock—it's my best. And I don't know what he said inside. He never told me. But I'll bet anything he didn't mean to cheat."

"You said lots of kind people would be ready to give money to get pudding for poor children. So I asked them to."

Oswald, with his strong right hand, waved a wave of passing things over.

"We'll talk about that another time," he said; "just now we've got weightier things to deal with."

He pointed to the pudding, which had grown cold during the conversation to which I have alluded. H.O. stopped crying, but Alice went on with it.

Oswald now said—

"We're a base and outcast family. Until that pudding's out of the house we shan't be able to look anyone in the face. We must see that that pudding goes to poor children—not grisling, grumpy, whiney-piney, pretending poor children—but real poor ones, just as poor as they can stick."

"And the figs too—and the dates," said Noël, with regretting tones.

"Every fig," said Dicky sternly. "Oswald is quite right."

This honorable resolution made us feel a bit better. We hastily put on our best things, and washed ourselves a bit, and hurried out to find some really poor people to give the pudding to. We cut it in slices ready, and put it in a basket with the figs and dates and toffee. We would not let H.O. come with us at first because he wanted to. And Alice would not come because of him. So at last we had to let him. The excitement of tearing into your best things heals the hurt that wounded honor feels, as the poetry writer said— or at any rate it makes the hurt feel better.

We went out into the streets. They were pretty quiet—nearly everybody was eating its Christmas dessert. But presently we met a woman in an apron. Oswald said very politely—

"Please, are you a poor person?" And she told us to get along with us. The next we met was a shabby man with a hole in his left boot.

Again Oswald said, "Please, are you a poor person, and have you any poor little children?"

The man told us not to come any of our games with him, or we should laugh on the wrong side of our faces. We went on sadly. We had no heart to stop and explain to him that we had no games to come.

The next was a young man near the Obelisk. Dora tried this time.

She said, "Oh, if you please we've got some Christmas pudding in this basket, and if you're a poor person you can have some."

"Poor as Job," said the young man in a hoarse voice, and he had to come up out of a red comforter to say it.

We gave him a slice of the pudding, and he bit into it without thanks or delay. The next minute he had thrown the pudding slap in Dora's face, and was clutching Dicky by the collar.

"Blime if I don't chuck ye in the river, the whole bloomin' lot of you!" he exclaimed.

The girls screamed, the boys shouted, and though Oswald threw himself on the insulter of his sister with all his manly vigor, yet but for a friend of Oswald's, who is in the police, passing at that instant, the author shudders to think what might have happened, for he was a strong young man, and Oswald is not yet come to his full strength, and the Quaggy runs all too near.

Our policeman led our assailant aside, and we waited anxiously, as he told us to. After long uncertain moments the young man in the comforter loafed off grumbling, and our policeman turned to us.

"Said you give him a dollop o' pudding, and it tasted of soap and hair-oil."

I suppose the hair-oil must have been the Brown Windsoriness of the soap coming out. We were sorry, but it was still our duty to get rid of the pudding. The Quaggy was handy, it is true, but when you have collected money to feed poor children and spent it on pudding it is not right to throw that pudding in the river. People do not subscribe shillings and sixpences and half-crowns to feed a hungry flood with Christmas pudding.

Yet we shrank from asking any more people whether they were poor persons, or about their families, and still more from offering the pudding to chance people who might bite into it and taste the soap before we had time to get away.

It was Alice, the most paralyzed with disgrace of all of us, who thought of the best idea.

She said, "Let's take it to the workhouse. At any rate they're all poor people there, and they mayn't go out without leave, so they can't run after us to do anything to us after the pudding. No one would give them leave to go out to pursue people who had brought them pudding, and wreck vengeance on them, and at any rate we shall get rid of the conscience-pudding—it's a sort of conscience-money, you know—only it isn't money but pudding."

The workhouse is a good way, but we stuck to it, though very cold, and hungrier than we thought possible when we started, for we had been so agitated we had not even stayed to eat the plain pudding our good Father had so kindly and thoughtfully ordered for our Christmas dinner.

The big bell at the workhouse made a man open the door to us, when we rang it. Oswald said (and he spoke because he is next eldest to Dora, and she had had jolly well enough of saying anything about pudding) he said—

"Please we've brought some pudding for the poor people."

He looked us up and down, and he looked at our basket, then he said: "You'd better see the Matron."

We waited in a hall, feeling more and more uncomfy, and less and less like Christmas. We were very cold indeed, especially our hands and our noses. And we felt less and less able to face the Matron if she was horrid, and one of us at least wished we had chosen the Quaggy for the pudding's long home, and made it up to the robbed poor in some other way afterwards.

Just as Alice was saying earnestly in the burning cold ear of Oswald, "Let's put down the basket and make a bolt for it. Oh, Oswald, let's!" a lady came along the passage. She was very upright, and she had eyes that went through you like blue gimlets. I should not like to be obliged to thwart that lady if she had any design, and mine was opposite. I am glad this is not likely to occur.

She said, "What's all this about a pudding?"

H.O. said at once, before we could stop him, "They say I've stolen the pudding, so we've brought it here for the poor people."

"No, we didn't!" "That wasn't why!" "The money was given!" "It was meant for the poor!" "Shut up, H.O.!" said the rest of us all at once.

Then there was an awful silence. The lady gimleted us again one by one with her blue eyes.

Then she said: "Come into my room. You all look frozen."

She took us into a very jolly room with velvet curtains and a big fire, and the gas lighted, because now it was almost dark, even out of doors. She gave us chairs, and Oswald felt as if his was a dock, he felt so criminal, and the lady looked so Judgular.

Then she took the arm-chair by the fire herself, and said, "Who's the eldest?"

"I am," said Dora, looking more like a frightened white rabbit than I've ever seen her.

"Then tell me all about it."

Dora looked at Alice and began to cry. That slab of pudding in the face had totally unnerved the gentle girl. Alice's eyes were red, and her face was puffy with crying; but she spoke up for Dora and said—

"Oh, please let Oswald tell. Dora can't. She's tired with the long walk. And a young man threw a piece of it in her face, and—"

The lady nodded and Oswald began. He told the story from the very beginning, as he has always been taught to, though he hated to lay bare the family honor's wound before a stranger, however judgelike and gimlet-eyed. He told all—not concealing the pudding-throwing, nor what the young man said about soap.

"So," he ended, "we want to give the conscience-pudding to you. It's like conscience-money, you know what that is, don't you? But if you really think it is soapy and not just the young man's horridness, perhaps you'd better not let them eat it. But the figs and things are all right."

When he had done the lady said, for most of us were crying more or less—

"Come, cheer up! It's Christmas-time, and he's very little your brother, I mean. And I think the rest of you seem pretty well able to take care of the honor of the family. I'll take the conscience-pudding off your minds. Where are you going now?"

"Home, I suppose," Oswald said. And he thought how nasty and dark and dull it would be. The fire out most likely and Father away.

"And your Father's not at home, you say," the blue-gimlet lady went on. "What do you say to having tea with me, and then seeing the entertainment we have got up for our old people?" Then the lady smiled and the blue gimlets looked quite merry. The room was so warm and comfortable and the invitation was the last thing we expected. It was jolly of her, I do think.

No one thought quite at first of saying how pleased we should be to accept her kind invitation. Instead we all just said "Oh!" but in a tone which must have told her we meant "Yes, please," very deeply.

Oswald (this has more than once happened) was the first to restore his manners. He made a proper bow like he has been taught, and said—

"Thank you very much. We should like it very much. It is very much nicer than going home. Thank you very much."

I need not tell the reader that Oswald could have made up a much better speech if he had had more time to make it up in, or if he had not been so filled with mixed flusteredness and furification by the shameful events of the day.

We washed our faces and hands and had a first rate muffin and crumpet tea, with slices of cold meats, and many nice jams and cakes. A lot of other people were there, most of them people who were giving the entertainment to the aged poor. After tea it was the entertainment. Songs and conjuring and a play called "Box and Cox," very amusing, and a lot of throwing things about in it—bacon and chops and things—and minstrels. We clapped till our hands were sore.

When it was over we said goodbye. In between the songs and things Oswald had had time to make up a speech of thanks to the lady.

He said—

"We all thank you heartily for your goodness. The entertainment was beautiful. We shall never forget your kindness and hospitableness."

The lady laughed, and said she had been very pleased to have us. A fat gentleman said—

"And your teas? I hope you enjoyed those—eh?"

Oswald had not had time to make up an answer to that, so he answered straight from the heart, and said—

"Ra—ther!"

And everyone laughed and slapped us boys on the back and kissed the girls, and the gentleman who played the bones in the minstrel show saw us home. We ate the cold pudding that night, and H.O. dreamed that something came to eat him, like it advises you to in the advertisements on the hoardings. The grown-ups said it was the pudding, but I don't think it could have been that, because, as I have said more than once, it was so very plain.

Some of H.O.'s brothers and sisters thought it was a judgment on him for pretending about who the poor children were he was collecting the money for. Oswald does not believe such a little boy as H.O. would have a real judgment made just for him and nobody else, whatever he did. But it certainly is odd. H.O. was the only one who had bad dreams, and he was also the only one who got any of the things we bought with that ill-gotten money, because, you remember, he picked a hole in the raisin-paper as he was bringing the parcel home. The rest of us had nothing, unless you count the scrapings of the pudding-basin, and those don't really count at all.

Christmas Chuckles

Sprinkle it Around

A lady was passing along the street one frosty Christmas morning and saw a little fellow scattering salt upon the pavement, for the purpose of melting the ice.

"Well, I'm sure," said the lady, "that's real benevolence."

"Oh, no, ma'am," he replied. "It ain't benevolence, it's salt."

Eli's Baby Story

"Lillie, did you say your prayers last night?" asked a fashionable mother of her sweet little girl who had remained home while the mother went to a Christmas ball.

"Yes, mamma, I said 'em all alone."

"But who did you say them to, Lillie, when your nurse was out with me?"

"Well, mamma, when I went to bed I looked around the house for somebody to say my prayers to, and there wasn't nobody in the house to say 'em to, and so I said 'em to God."

Christmas Carols

Next 2 pages. Sing the two Christmas Carols together as a family. Discuss what the songs mean.

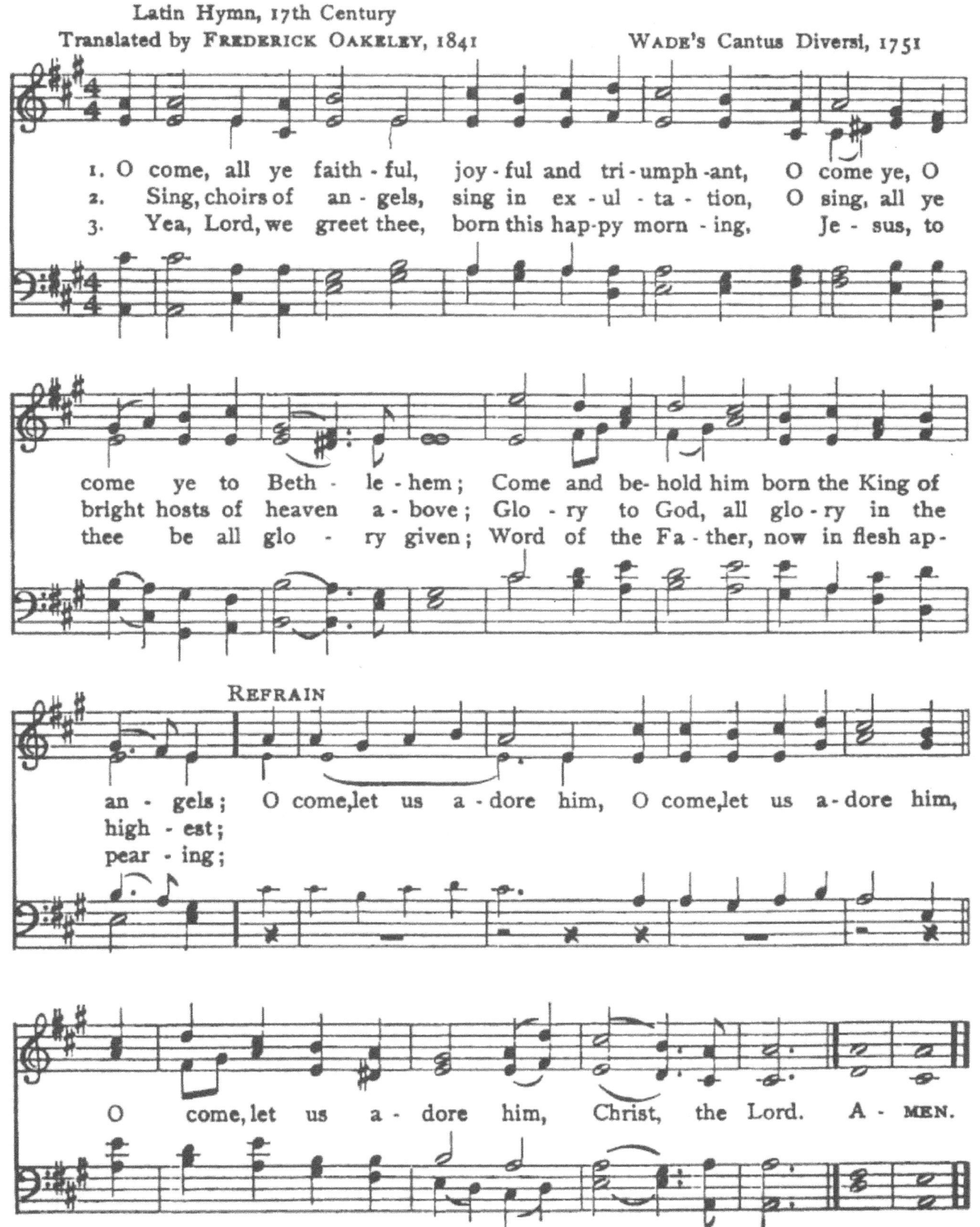

December 6

Saint Nicholas
Adapted by Amy Puetz Fox
from an original by Robert Chambers

Who was Saint Nicholas? Did he really live? So many legends have sprung up about Saint Nicholas or Santa Clause as we know him in the United States. Let's look at the real story behind the man. ~Amy

St. Nicholas belongs to the fourth century of the Christian era, and was a native of the city of Patara, in Lycia, in Asia Minor. So strong were his devotional tendencies, even from infancy, that we are gravely informed that he refused to nurse on Wednesdays and Fridays, the fast-days appointed by the church! Having embraced a religious life by entering the monastery of Sion, near Myra, he was, in course of time, raised to the dignity of abbot, and for many years made himself conspicuous by acts of piety and benevolence. Subsequently, he was elected archbishop of the metropolitan church of Myra, and exercised that office with great renown until his death. Though escaping actual martyrdom, he is said to have suffered imprisonment, and otherwise testified to the faith under the persecution of Diocletian.

Perhaps no saint has enjoyed a more extended popularity than St Nicholas. By the Russian nation, he has been adopted as their patron, and in England no fewer than three hundred and seventy-two churches are named in his honor. He is regarded as the special guardian of virgins, of children, and of sailors. Scholars were under his protection, and from the circumstance of these being anciently denominated clerks, the fraternity of parish clerks placed themselves likewise under the guardianship of St Nicholas. He even came to be regarded as the patron of robbers, from an alleged adventure with thieves, whom he compelled to restore some stolen goods to their proper owners. But there are two specially celebrated legends regarding this saint, one of which bears reference to his protectorship of virgins, and the other to that of children. The former of these stories is as follows: A nobleman in the town of Patara had three daughters, but was sunk in such poverty, that he was not only unable to provide them with suitable marriage-portions, but was on the point of abandoning them to a sinful course of life from inability to preserve them otherwise from starvation. St Nicholas, who had inherited a large fortune, and employed it in numerable acts of charity, no sooner heard of this unfortunate family, than he resolved to save it from the degradation with which it was threatened. As he proceeded secretly to the nobleman's house at night, debating with himself how he might best accomplish his object, the moon shone out from behind a cloud, and showed him an open window into which he threw a purse of gold. This fell at the feet of the father of the maidens, and enabled him to provide a dowry for his eldest daughter. A second night-time visit was paid to the house by the saint, and a similar present bestowed, which procured a dowry for the second daughter of the nobleman. But the latter was now determined to discover his mysterious benefactor, and with that view set himself to watch. On St Nicholas' approaching, and preparing to throw in a purse of money for the third daughter, the nobleman caught hold of the skirt of his robe, and threw himself at his feet, exclaiming: "O Nicholas! Servant of God! Why seek to hide thyself?" But the saint made him promise that he would inform no one of this seasonable act of benevolence. From this incident in his life is derived apparently the practice of the elder members and friends of a family placing, on the eve of St Nicholas's Day, little presents, such as sweetmeats and similar gifts, in the shoes or stocking of their younger relatives, who, on discovering them in the morning, are supposed to attribute them to the bounty of St Nicholas.

The second legend to which we have adverted is even of a more piquant nature. A gentleman of Asia sent his two sons to be educated at Athens, but desired them, in passing through the town of Myra, to call on its archbishop, the holy Nicholas, and receive his benediction. The young men, arriving at the town late in the evening, resolved to defer their visit till the morning, and in the meantime took up their abode at an inn. The landlord, in order to obtain possession of their baggage, murdered the unfortunate youths in their sleep. But the archbishop was warned by a vision of this horrid transaction, and proceeded immediately to the inn, where he charged the landlord with the crime. The man, finding himself discovered, confessed his guilt, with great contrition, to St Nicholas, who implored on his behalf the forgiveness of Heaven. St. Nicholas made the sign of the cross over the dead bodies and offered up a supplication for their restoration to life. Scarcely was the saint's prayer finished, when the two youths regaining animation, rose up alive, and threw themselves at the feet of their benefactor. We are further informed that the archbishop refused their homage, desiring the young men to return thanks to the proper quarter from which this blessing had descended; and then, after giving them his benediction, he dismissed them with great joy to continue their journey to Athens.

Christmas Celebration in Other Countries*

In Belgium and Holland, Saint Nicholas Day (December 6) is still the day of joy and not Christmas. "On the eve of his festival day," writes an authority, "Saint Nicholas makes his tour, visiting palace and cottage. Frequently in the early evening he makes a preliminary visit in his bishop's robes, with pastoral staff and mitre, at each house, making inquiries concerning the conduct of the children, giving appropriate praise or warning, and promising on the following morning to give substantial reward. When he is gone, the children place receptacles for the gifts which Saint Nicholas is expected to let fall down the chimney. The vessel varies in different places. Sometimes shoes are neatly polished for the purpose. At other times plates, baskets, stockings, or specially-made shoes of porcelain are set on the bed, in the open chimney, before the door of a room, or merely in the corner of a room. Saint Nicholas' steed, variously conceived of as a gray horse or a white ass, is not forgotten. For him the children put water and hay, carrot, potato peeling, or a piece of bread in the shoe, basket, or stocking. In the morning from the tipped-over chairs and general disarray in the room it is evident that Saint Nicholas has been present. Replacing the oats, hay, or carrot are found sweets and playthings for children that have been good, obedient, and studious during the year. In the case of bad children, rods are left and the fodder is untouched."

Saint Nicholas' robe—his "tabard"—enables him to travel from place to place instantly. In Holland he is supposed to use a horse for his journey at night over the roofs of the houses. Belgium and Holland have special cakes and sweets for the Saint Nicholas season. Life-sized figures of Saint Nicholas are often placed in front of shop windows and in some places a man dressed like the saint goes about the streets with presents and on a white horse. The Dutch settlers brought the Saint Nicholas customs to New York, whence they spread to other parts of the United States and became combined with the Christmas customs from other countries. The American "Santa Claus" is a corruption of the Dutch San Nicolaas. "Santa Claus," writes George Harley McKnight,* "the name derived from Saint Nicholas through the familiar use of children in Teutonic countries, crossed to America. The exact route followed by him is somewhat open to question. On the way he traded his gray horse or donkey for a reindeer and made changes in his appearance. In America he has made himself very much at home; and, according to the explanation most generally accepted, from America he recrossed the Atlantic to England, whence he has journeyed to the most distant parts of the British Empire, to India, and to Australia, where he is as familiarly known as in America." The immortal poem of "The Night Before Christmas," by Clement C. Moore, makes him a jolly elf "Saint Nick," who rides "in a miniature sleigh drawn by eight tiny reindeer."

*Author of *St. Nicholas: His Legend and His Role in the Christmas Celebration and Other Popular Customs*

Christmas Games

Even or Odd?
By Laura Valentine

This game is the most ancient, I think, that we know. The children who played in the streets of Athens and in the Roman Forum in early ages knew and loved it, and little English children find amusement in it still. It is played in this manner: One child hides in his or her hand a few beans, nuts, almonds, or even bits of paper, and asks his or her companion to guess if they are odd or even.

If the playfellow guesses odd, and on opening his or her hand the other displays an odd number, he or she forfeits the articles to the guesser, who hides them in their turn; but if the guess is odd, and the number even, the guesser pays a forfeit, and the first hider retains the beans. The guess must be right to win.

Beans are Hot
By Laura Valentine

This is a hiding game. One player goes out of the room; the others hide something, which has been previously chosen for the purpose. It may be a fan, a ball, a card, a key, etc. When they have hidden it, they call their friend in, by saying at the door—

"Hot beans and melted butter!
Please, my friend, come to supper."

He or she instantly begins to search for the hidden thing, in the curtains, under the hearthrug, in the piano—everywhere, in short. When she approaches the right spot, the hiders cry, "Hot beans!" When he or she moves away from it, they cry, "Cold beans!"

If the searcher finds the concealed article, he or she hides it next time. If he or she gives up the search, the searcher pays a forfeit.

Sometimes a whole party goes out of the room, and one remains in it to hide the chosen object they are to seek.

When they return, she watches them and calls out who is "hot" or "cold" by name, as "Charley is growing warm," "Henry is quite hot," "Oh, now, Mary, you are so cold!"

"Hot" means near the hidden thing; "cold" means a great way off.

December 7

Why the Chimes Rang
By Raymond MacDonald Alden

There was once in a faraway country where few people have ever traveled, a wonderful church. It stood on a high hill in the midst of a great city; and every Sunday, as well as on sacred days like Christmas, thousands of people climbed the hill to its great archways, looking like lines of ants all moving in the same direction.

When you came to the building itself, you found stone columns and dark passages, and a grand entrance leading to the main room of the church. This room was so long that one standing at the doorway could scarcely see to the other end, where the choir stood by the marble altar. In the farthest corner was the organ; and this organ was so loud, that sometimes when it played, the people for miles around would close their shutters and prepare for a great thunderstorm. Altogether, no such church as this was ever seen before, especially when it was lighted up for some festival, and crowded with people, young and old. But the strangest thing about the whole building was the wonderful chime of bells.

At one corner of the church was a great gray tower, with ivy growing over it as far up as one could see. I say as far as one could see, because the tower was quite great enough to fit the great church, and it rose so far into the sky that it was only in very fair weather that anyone claimed to be able to see the top. Even then one could not be certain that it was in sight. Up, and up, and up climbed the stones and the ivy; and as the men who built the church had been dead for hundreds of years, everyone had forgotten how high the tower was supposed to be.

Now all the people knew that at the top of the tower was a chime of Christmas bells. They had hung there ever since the church had been built, and were the most beautiful bells in the world. Some thought it was because a great musician had cast them and arranged them in their place; others said it was because of the great height, which reached up where the air was clearest and purest; however that might be, no one who had ever heard the chimes denied that they were the sweetest in the world. Some described them as sounding like angels far up in the sky; others as sounding like strange winds singing through the trees.

But the fact was that no one had heard them for years and years. There was an old man living not far from the church who said that his mother had spoken of hearing them when she was a little girl, and he was the only one who was sure of as much as that. They were Christmas chimes, you see, and were not meant to be played by men or on common days. It was the custom on Christmas Eve for all the people to bring to the church their offerings to the Christ-Child; and when the greatest and best offering was laid on the altar there used to come sounding through the music of the choir the Christmas chimes far up in the tower. Some said that the wind rang them, and others, that they were so high that the angels could set them swinging. But for many long years they had never been heard.

It was said that people had been growing less careful of their gifts for the Christ-Child, and that no offering was brought great enough to deserve the music of the chimes.

Every Christmas Eve the rich people still crowded to the altar, each one trying to bring some better gift than any other, without giving anything that he wanted for himself, and the church was crowded with those who thought that perhaps the wonderful bells might be heard again. But although the service was splendid, and the offerings plenty, only the roar of the wind could be heard, far up in the stone tower.

Now, a number of miles from the city, in a little country village, where nothing could be seen of the great church but glimpses of the tower when the weather was fine, lived a boy named Pedro, and his little brother. They knew very little about the Christmas chimes, but they had heard of the service in the church on Christmas Eve, and had a secret plan which they had often talked over when by themselves, to go to see the beautiful celebration.

"Nobody can guess, Little Brother," Pedro would say; "all the fine things there are to see and hear; and I have even heard it said that the Christ-Child sometimes comes down to bless the service. What if we could see Him?"

The day before Christmas was bitterly cold, with a few lonely snowflakes flying in the air, and a hard white crust on the ground. Sure enough Pedro and Little Brother were able to slip quietly away early in the afternoon; and although the walking was hard in the frosty air, before nightfall they had trudged so far, hand in hand, that they saw the lights of the big city just ahead of them. Indeed they were about to enter one of the great gates in the wall that surrounded it, when they saw something dark on the snow near their path, and stepped aside to look at it.

It was a poor woman, who had fallen just outside the city, too sick and tired to get in where she might have found shelter. The soft drift of snow made a sort of pillow for her, and she would soon be so sound asleep, in the wintry air, that no one could ever waken her again. All this Pedro saw in a moment and he knelt down beside her and tried to rouse her, even tugging at her arm a little, as though he would have tried to carry her away. He turned her face toward him, so that he could rub some of the snow on it, and when he had looked at her silently a moment he stood up again, and said:

"It's no use, Little Brother. You will have to go on alone."

"Alone?" cried Little Brother. "And you not see the Christmas festival?"

"No," said Pedro, and he could not keep back a bit of a choking sound in his throat. "See this poor woman. Her face looks like the Madonna in the chapel window, and she will freeze to death if nobody cares for her. Everyone has gone to the church now, but when you come back you can bring someone to help her. I will rub her to keep her from freezing, and perhaps get her to eat the bun that is left in my pocket."

"But I cannot bear to leave you, and go on alone," said Little Brother.

"Both of us need not miss the service," said Pedro, "and it had better be I than you. You can easily find your way to church; and you must see and hear everything twice, Little Brother—once for you and once for me. I am sure the Christ-Child must know how I should love to come with you and worship Him; and oh! If you get a chance, Little Brother, to slip up to the altar without getting in anyone's way, take this little silver piece of mine, and lay it down for my offering, when no one is looking. Do not forget where you have left me, and forgive me for not going with you."

In this way he hurried Little Brother off to the city and winked hard to keep back the tears, as he heard the crunching footsteps sounding farther and farther away in the twilight. It was pretty hard to lose the music and splendor of the Christmas celebration that he had been planning for so long, and spend the time instead in that lonely place in the snow.

The great church was a wonderful place that night. Everyone said that it had never looked so bright and beautiful before. When the organ played and the thousands of people sang, the walls shook with the sound, and little Pedro, away outside the city wall, felt the earth tremble around them.

At the close of the service came the procession with the offerings to be laid on the altar. Rich men and great men marched proudly up to lay down their gifts to the Christ-Child. Some brought wonderful jewels, some baskets of gold so heavy that they could scarcely carry them down the aisle. A great writer laid down a book that he had been making for years and years. And last of all walked the king of the country, hoping with all the rest to win for himself the chime of the Christmas bells. There went a great murmur through the church as the people saw the king take from his head the royal crown, all set with precious stones, and lay it gleaming on the altar, as his offering to the Holy Child. "Surely," everyone said, "we shall hear the bells now, for nothing like this has ever happened before."

But still only the cold old wind was heard in the tower and the people shook their heads; and some of them said, as they had before, that they never really believed the story of the chimes, and doubted if they ever rang at all.

The procession was over, and the choir began the closing hymn. Suddenly the organist stopped playing; and everyone looked at the old minister, who was standing by the altar, holding up his hand for silence. Not a sound could be heard from anyone in the church, but as all the people strained their ears to listen, there came softly, but distinctly, swinging through the air, the sound of the chimes in the tower. So far away, and yet so clear the music seemed—so much sweeter were the notes than anything that had been heard before, rising and falling away up there in the sky, that the people in the church sat for a moment as still as though something held each of them by the shoulders. Then they all stood up together and stared straight at the altar, to see what great gift had awakened the long silent bells.

But all that the nearest of them saw was the childish figure of Little Brother, who had crept softly down the aisle when no one was looking, and had laid Pedro's little piece of silver on the altar.

Christmas Traditions
The Origin of the Christmas Stocking

From Italy comes the legend from which we get the time-honored custom of hanging up the Christmas stocking. Good old St. Nicholas of Myra used to throw long knitted purses, tied at both ends, into the open windows of the very poor people; these purses were of yarn and not unlike a footless stocking. Finally it became the custom of the people to hang these long empty receptacles out of their windows on the night before Christmas, so that St. Nicholas could put a gift into them as he passed by. By and by, when coin became scarce, toys were put in for the children, and useful presents for grown people. In the north country, where it was rather chilly at Christmas time, the purses were hung on the mantelpiece, and it was believed that the good old Saint would come down the chimney and fill them. When these purses went out of use, stockings were substituted and have been used ever since.

Riddles
by Melville De Lancey Landon and Mark Twain

1. My first is a game; my second is what we use our eyes for; my whole is one of the United States. (Tennes see)

2. At evening by my whole you'll think of days gone by; and never reckon that by my second my first is made, and by my first my second (Fire light)

3. My first makes all nature appear with one face;
My second has music and beauty and grace;
My whole, when the winter hangs dull o'er the earth,
Is a source of much pleasure of mischief and mirth. (Snow-ball)

4. Dear is my first when shadowy night is near,
It is my second makes my first so dear;
My whole with decent care my first preserves,
And thus to be my second well deserves. (House-wife)

5. My first is on the reindeer's head,
My second is a measure,
My total is a favorite dance,
That's always seen with pleasure. (Horn-pipe)

6. My first brings joy to all around, my second may bring sorrow,
My whole but once a year is found, and may be yours tomorrow. (Birth-day)

7. What is that which you have, and everybody has at the same time? (A name)

8. Without my first my second could never have existed, and my whole is as old as creation. (Sun-day)

9. Round the house, round the house, and leaves a white glove in the window? (Snow)

10. What is that which by adding something to it will become smaller, but if you add nothing it will grow larger? (A hole in a stocking)

11. There is a thing that nothing is,
And yet it has a name;
'Tis sometimes tall and sometimes short,
It joins our walks, it joins our sport,
And plays at every game. (A shadow)

December 8

Christmas Every Day
By W.D. Howells

The little girl came into her papa's study, as she always did Saturday morning before breakfast, and asked for a story. He tried to beg off that morning, for he was very busy, but she would not let him. So he began:

"Well, once there was a little pig—"

She put her hand over his mouth and stopped him at the word. She said she had heard little pig-stories till she was perfectly sick of them.

"Well, what kind of story shall I tell, then?"

"About Christmas. It's getting to be the season. It's past Thanksgiving already."

"It seems to me," her papa argued, "that I've told as often about Christmas as I have about little pigs."

"No difference! Christmas is more interesting."

"Well!" Her papa roused himself from his writing by a great effort. "Well, then, I'll tell you about the little girl that wanted it Christmas every day in the year. How would you like that?"

"First-rate!" said the little girl; and she nestled into comfortable shape in his lap, ready for listening.

"Very well, then, this little pig—Oh, what are you pounding me for?"

"Because you said little pig instead of little girl."

"I should like to know what's the difference between a little pig and a little girl that wanted it Christmas every day!"

"Papa," said the little girl, warningly, "if you don't go on, I'll give it to you!" And at this her papa darted off like lightning, and began to tell the story as fast as he could.

Well, once there was a little girl who liked Christmas so much that she wanted it to be Christmas every day in the year; and as soon as Thanksgiving was over she began to send postal-cards to the old Christmas Fairy to ask if she mightn't have it. But the old fairy never answered any of the postals; and after a while the little girl found out that the Fairy was pretty particular, and wouldn't notice anything but letters—not even correspondence cards in envelopes; but real letters on sheets of paper, and sealed outside with a monogram—or your initial, anyway. So, then, she began to send her letters; and in about three weeks—or just the day before Christmas, it was—she got a letter from the Fairy, saying she might have Christmas every day for a year, and then they would see about having it longer.

The little girl was a good deal excited already, preparing for the old-fashioned, once-a-year Christmas that was coming the next day, and perhaps the Fairy's promise didn't make such an impression on her as it would have made at some other time. She just resolved to keep it to herself, and surprise everybody with it as it kept coming true; and then it slipped out of her mind altogether.

She had a splendid Christmas. She went to bed early, so as to let Santa Claus have a chance at the stockings, and in the morning she was up the first of anybody and went and felt them, and found hers all lumpy with packages of candy, and oranges and grapes, and pocket-books and rubber balls, and all kinds of small presents, and her big brother's with nothing but the tongs in them, and her young lady sister's with a new silk umbrella, and her papa's and mamma's with potatoes and pieces of coal wrapped up in tissue-paper, just as they always had every Christmas. Then she waited around till the rest of the family were up, and she was the first to burst into the library, when the doors were opened, and look at the large presents laid out on the library-table—books, and portfolios, and boxes of stationery, and breastpins, and dolls, and little stoves, and dozens of handkerchiefs, and ink-stands, and skates, and snow-shovels, and photograph-frames, and little easels, and boxes of water-colors, and Turkish paste, and nougat, and candied cherries, and dolls' houses, and waterproofs—and the big Christmas-tree, lighted and standing in a waste-basket in the middle.

She had a splendid Christmas all day. She ate so much candy that she did not want any breakfast; and the whole forenoon the presents kept pouring in that the expressman had not had time to deliver the night before; and she went round giving the presents she had got for other people, and came home and ate turkey and cranberry for dinner, and plum-pudding and nuts and raisins and oranges and more candy, and then went out and coasted, and came in with a stomachache, crying; and her papa said he would see if his house was turned into that sort of fool's paradise another year; and they had a light supper, and pretty early everybody went to bed cross.

Here the little girl pounded her papa in the back, again.

"Well, what now? Did I say pigs?"

"You made them act like pigs."

"Well, didn't they?"

"No matter; you oughtn't to put it into a story."

"Very well, then, I'll take it all out."

Her father went on:

The little girl slept very heavily, and she slept very late, but she was wakened at last by the other children dancing round her bed with their stockings full of presents in their hands.

"What is it?" said the little girl, and she rubbed her eyes and tried to rise up in bed.

"Christmas! Christmas! Christmas!" they all shouted, and waved their stockings.

"Nonsense! It was Christmas yesterday."

Her brothers and sisters just laughed. "We don't know about that. It's Christmas today, anyway. You come into the library and see."

Then all at once it flashed on the little girl that the Fairy was keeping her promise, and her year of Christmases was beginning. She was dreadfully sleepy, but she sprang up like a lark—a lark that had overeaten itself and gone to bed cross—and darted into the library. There it was again! Books, and portfolios, and boxes of stationery, and breastpins—

"You needn't go over it all, papa; I guess I can remember just what was there," said the little girl.

Well, and there was the Christmas tree blazing away, and the family picking out their presents, but looking pretty sleepy, and her father perfectly puzzled, and her mother ready to cry. "I'm sure I don't see how I'm to dispose of all these things," said her mother, and her father said it seemed to him they had had something just like it the day before, but he supposed he must have dreamed it. This struck the little girl as the best kind of a joke; and so she ate so much candy she didn't want any breakfast, and went round carrying presents, and had turkey and cranberry for dinner, and then went out and coasted, and came in with a—

"Papa!"

"Well, what now?"

"What did you promise, you forgetful thing?"

"Oh! Oh yes!"

Well, the next day, it was just the same thing over again, but everybody getting crosser; and at the end of a week's time so many people had lost their tempers that you could pick up lost tempers anywhere; they perfectly strewed the ground. Even when people tried to recover their tempers they usually got somebody else's, and it made the most dreadful mix.

The little girl began to get frightened, keeping the secret all to herself; she wanted to tell her mother, but she didn't dare to; and she was ashamed to ask the Fairy to take back her gift, it seemed ungrateful and ill-bred, and she thought she would try to stand it, but she hardly knew how she could, for a whole year. So it went on and on, and it was Christmas on St. Valentine's Day and Washington's Birthday, just the same as any day, and it didn't skip even the First of April, though everything was counterfeit that day, and that was some little relief.

After a while coal and potatoes began to be awfully scarce, so many had been wrapped up in tissue paper to fool papas and mammas with. Turkeys got to be about a thousand dollars apiece—

"Papa!"

"Well, what?"

"You're beginning to fib."

"Well, two thousand, then."

And they got to passing off almost anything for turkeys—half-grown humming-birds, and even rocs out of the Arabian Nights—the real turkeys were so scarce. And cranberries—well, they asked a diamond apiece for cranberries. All the woods and orchards were cut down for Christmas trees, and where the woods and orchards used to be it looked just like a stubble-field, with the stumps. After a while they had to make Christmas trees out of rags, and stuff them with bran, like old-fashioned dolls; but there were plenty of rags, because people got so poor, buying presents for one another, that they couldn't get any new clothes, and they just wore their old ones to tatters. They got so poor that everybody had to go to the poor-house, except the confectioners, and the fancy-store keepers, and the picture-book sellers, and the expressmen; and they all got so rich and proud that they would hardly wait upon a person when he came to buy. It was perfectly shameful!

Well, after it had gone on about three or four months, the little girl, whenever she came into the room in the morning and saw those great ugly, lumpy stockings dangling at the fireplace, and the disgusting presents around everywhere, used to just sit down and burst out crying. In six months she was perfectly exhausted; she couldn't even cry anymore; she just lay on the lounge and rolled her eyes and panted. About the beginning of October she took to sitting down on dolls wherever she found them—French dolls, or any kind—she hated the sight of them so; and by Thanksgiving she was crazy, and just slammed her presents across the room.

By that time people didn't carry presents around nicely any more. They flung them over the fence, or through the window, or anything; and, instead of running their tongues out and taking great pains to write "For dear Papa," or "Mamma," or "Brother," or "Sister," or "Susie," or "Sammie," or "Billie," or "Bobbie," or "Jimmie," or "Jennie," or whoever it was, and troubling to get the spelling right, and then signing their names, and "Xmas, 18—," they used to write in the gift-books, "Take it, you horrid old thing!" and then go and bang it against the front door. Nearly everybody had built barns to hold their presents, but pretty soon the barns overflowed, and then they used to let them lie out in the rain, or anywhere. Sometimes the police used to come and tell them to shovel their presents off the sidewalk, or they would arrest them.

"I thought you said everybody had gone to the poor-house," interrupted he little girl.

"They did go, at first," said her papa; "but after a while the poor-houses got so full that they had to send the people back to their own houses. They tried to cry, when they got back, but they couldn't make the least sound."

"Why couldn't they?"

"Because they had lost their voices, saying 'Merry Christmas' so much. Did I tell you how it was on the Fourth of July?"

"No; how was it?" And the little girl nestled closer, in expectation of something uncommon.

Well, the night before, the boys stayed up to celebrate, as they always do, and fell asleep before twelve o'clock, as usual, expecting to be wakened by the bells and cannon. But it was nearly eight o'clock before the first boy in the United States woke up, and then he found out what the trouble was. As soon as he could get his clothes on he ran out of the house and smashed a big cannon-torpedo down on the pavement; but it didn't make any more noise than a damp wad of paper; and after he tried about twenty or thirty more, he began to pick them up and look at them. Every single torpedo was a big raisin! Then he just streaked it upstairs, and examined his firecrackers and toy-pistol and two-dollar collection of fireworks, and found that they were nothing but sugar and candy painted up to look like fireworks! Before ten o'clock every boy in the United States found out that his Fourth of July things had turned into Christmas things; and then they just sat down and cried—they were so mad. There are about twenty million boys in the United States, and so you can imagine what a noise they made. Some men got together before night, with a little powder that hadn't turned into purple sugar yet, and they said they would fire off one cannon, anyway. But the cannon burst into a thousand pieces, for it was nothing but rock-candy, and some of the men nearly got killed. The Fourth of July orations all turned into Christmas carols, and when anybody tried to read the Declaration, instead of saying, "When in the course of human events it becomes necessary," he was sure to sing, "God rest you, merry gentlemen." It was perfectly awful.

The little girl drew a deep sigh of satisfaction. "And how was it at Thanksgiving?"

Her papa hesitated. "Well, I'm almost afraid to tell you. I'm afraid you'll think it's wicked."

"Well, tell, anyway," said the little girl.

Well, before it came Thanksgiving it had leaked out who had caused all these Christmases. The little girl had suffered so much that she had talked about it in her sleep; and after that hardly anybody would play with her. People just perfectly despised her, because if it had not been for her greediness it wouldn't have happened; and now, when it came Thanksgiving, and she wanted them to go to church, and have squash-pie and turkey, and show their gratitude, they said that all the turkeys had been eaten up for her old Christmas dinners, and if she would stop the Christmases, they would see about the gratitude. Wasn't it dreadful? And the very next day the little girl began to send letters to the Christmas Fairy, and then telegrams, to stop it. But it didn't do any good; and then she got to calling at the Fairy's house, but the girl that came to the door always said, "Not at home," or "Engaged," or "At dinner," or something like that; and so it went on till it came to the old once-a-year Christmas Eve. The little girl fell asleep, and when she woke up in the morning—

"She found it was all nothing but a dream," suggested the little girl.

"No, indeed!" said her papa. "It was all every bit true!"

"Well, what did she find out, then?"

"Why, that it wasn't Christmas at last, and wasn't ever going to be, any more. Now it's time for breakfast."

The little girl held her papa fast around the neck.

"You sha'n't go if you're going to leave it so!"

"How do you want it left?"

"Christmas once a year."

"All right," said her papa; and he went on again.

Well, there was the greatest rejoicing all over the country, and it extended clear up into Canada. The people met together everywhere, and kissed and cried for joy. The city carts went around and gathered up all the candy and raisins and nuts, and dumped them into the river; and it made the fish perfectly sick; and the whole United States, as far out as Alaska, was one blaze of bonfires, where the children were burning up their gift-books and presents of all kinds. They had the greatest time!

The little girl went to thank the old Fairy because she had stopped its being Christmas, and she said she hoped she would keep her promise and see that Christmas never, never came again. Then the Fairy frowned, and asked her if she was sure she knew what she meant; and the little girl asked her, Why not? And the old Fairy said that now she was behaving just as greedily as ever, and she'd better look out. This made the little girl think it all over carefully again, and she said she would be willing to have it Christmas about once in a thousand years; and then she said a hundred, and then she said ten, and at last she got down to one. Then the Fairy said that was the good old way that had pleased people ever since Christmas began, and she was agreed. Then the little girl said, "What're your shoes made of?" And the Fairy said, "Leather." And the little girl said, "Bargain's done forever," and skipped off, and hippity-hopped the whole way home, she was so glad.

"How will that do?" asked the papa.

"First-rate!" said the little girl; but she hated

to have the story stop, and was rather sober. However, her mamma put her head in at the door, and asked her papa:

"Are you never coming to breakfast? What have you been telling that child?"

"Oh, just a moral tale."

The little girl caught him around the neck again.

"We know! Don't you tell what, papa! Don't you tell what!"

A Candlemas Dialogue
by Christina Rossetti

"Love brought Me down;
and cannot love make thee
Carol for joy to Me?
Hear cheerful robin carol from his tree,
Who owes not half to Me
I won for thee."

"Yea, Lord, I hear his carol's wordless voice;
And well may he rejoice
Who hath not heard of death's
discordant noise.
So might I too rejoice
With such a voice."

"True, thou hast compassed death;
but hast not thou
The tree of life's own bough?
Am I not Life and Resurrection
now?
My Cross balm-bearing bough
For such as thou?"

"Ah me, Thy Cross!—but that seems far
away;
Thy Cradle-song today
I too would raise, and worship Thee and pray:
Not empty, Lord, today
Send me away."

"If thou wilt not go empty, spend thy store;
And I will give thee more,
Yea, make thee ten times richer than before.
Give more and give yet more
Out of thy store."

"Because Thou givest me Thyself,
I will Thy blessed word fulfill,
Give with both hands,
and hoard by giving still;
Thy pleasure to fulfill,
And work Thy Will."

Christmas Craft

Christmas Cards Bag *by Lina Beard and Adelia Belle Beard*

Scrap-bags have been fashioned in many shapes and sizes and of all sorts of material, still it remains to be shown in what manner Christmas cards may add in decoration and beauty to these useful articles. From your collection of Christmas cards choose four of the same size. Cut off the front of the cards. Sew the cards on a piece of bright silk or cloth at equal distances apart (as in Fig. 1), stitching them around the edges on the sewing machine. At the dotted line, fold over the top of the bag as if for a hem, making the narrow fold lap just cover the upper edge of the cards; stitch this down to form a binding.

After joining the bag at the dotted lines on the sides, gather the bottom up tight and fasten a good-sized tassel to the bottom. Sew a heavy cord with tassels on two sides, placing them where the cord joins the bag as seen in Fig. 2. The cord and tassels of the example were made of scarlet worsted.

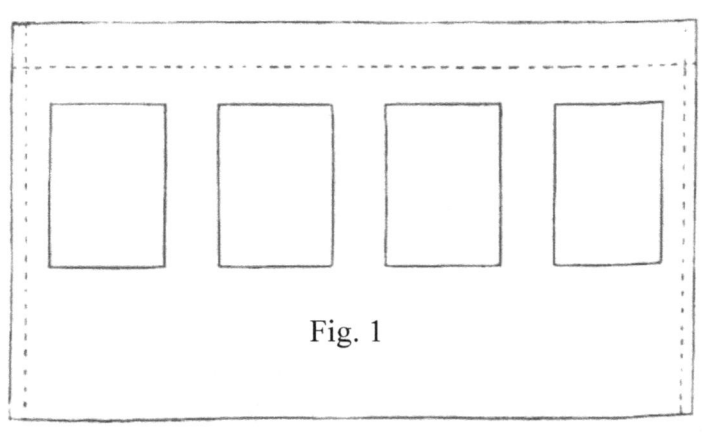

Fig. 1

Fig. 2

A Walnut-Shell Turtle *by Lina Beard and Adelia Belle Beard*

For an ornament to be used on a pen-wiper, or simply as a pretty toy, the little turtle is appropriate. It is made of half an English walnut, which forms the turtle's back or shell, glued on a piece of cardboard cut after the diagram given in Fig. 3. Paint the cardboard as nearly as possible the color of the shell, and the eyes black. When perfectly dry, glue the shell securely to the cardboard. Bend the feet down and slightly out to make the turtle stand. Bend the head up and the tail down as in Fig. 4.

Fig. 3

Fig. 4

December 9

Wenceslas
By Amy Puetz Fox

"What a fine man he will make someday," the kind duke said affectionately as he held a wee babe in his strong arms. The man beamed at his brother, the father of the child. "It was good of you to invite me, brother," Wenceslas said in his friendly and caring manner. "I share the joy of your firstborn son."

Wenceslas rocked the baby in his arms and thought about his own pride at being a father, and about how his father must have been doubly pleased at the birth of Wenceslas and his twin brother Boleslav over twenty years earlier. Now, it seemed that Boleslav was eager to be on friendly terms again. The good duke said a silent prayer that his younger brother would embrace the Christian faith. Then he thought back to the events that had brought him to his brother's castle at Stara-Boleslav in Bohemia (the modern-day Czech Republic).

When he and his brother were born about 907 AD, Christianity had only recently spread its light into the land of Bohemia. Through the missionary work of Cyril and Methodius, Wenceslas's grandparents Borivoy and Ludmilla were converted. Although his father Vratislav (or Ratislav) also became a follower of Jesus Christ, he married a pagan princess named Drahomira. Outwardly, Wenceslas's mother pretended to be a Christian, but her true colors showed after the death of her husband.

The childhood of Wenceslas was spent happily at his grandmother's castle in Tetin. Through her dedicated teaching, he learned about Christian virtue, love, and self-sacrifice, but most importantly, about Jesus Christ. For a time he attended a school at Budec—the first Latin school in Bohemia—where he learned Latin, science, and other subjects. His education prepared him to become the next duke of Bohemia, a position that was vacated all too soon with the untimely death of his father. Sometime around 916, Vratislav was slain in battle. Since Wenceslas was underage, his mother became regent.

Now that power was in her hands, she returned to pagan worship. Fierce persecution was unleashed on priests and other Christians. Fearing Ludmilla's influence over Wenceslas, Drahomira brought him back to her castle at Prague and tried to persuade him to embrace the pagan religion. Her plans were unfruitful.

Despite the fact that Drahomira held the power, she still feared Ludmilla's influence on her son and the country. Ludmilla was determined to keep the Christian faith. In about 921, several of Drahomira's agents went to Ludmilla's castle at Tetin and strangled her to death with the veil she was wearing.

The cruel murder of his beloved grandmother led Wenceslas to overthrow his mother and her pagan followers. It would have been natural for Wenceslas to execute his mother for her devilish deeds, but his mercy guided him. Instead of having Drahomira put to death, Wenceslas exiled her and his brother, Boleslav. His Christian example of forgiveness made a good impression on the Christians of Bohemia, but it did nothing to soften his mother's heart.

Wenceslas's rule as duke began about 922. A kinder ruler never lived! He took a genuine interest in the lives of his subjects and worked for the good of his kingdom. When Radislas, a duke from a neighboring country, attempted to invade Bohemia, Wenceslas challenged him to single combat. He knew a battle would cause the loss of many lives while a dual between two men could determine the fate of the nation with only one death. During the fight, Wenceslas was not well armed, and it should have been an easy victory for Radislas, but Wenceslas had right on his side, and it is said that angels protected him. The overconfident Radislas begged pardon of the generous Wenceslas and went away in peace.

The noble deeds of Wenceslas were so numerous that it would take a long time to tell them all. He cared for the poor, redeemed captives, built churches, and in every way exemplified Christian virtue. If he had not been of royal blood, it is possible that he might have become a priest or a monk, because he was so devoted to the ways of God. He even helped cultivate the grain and grapes that were used in Holy Communion.

It is because of his benevolent spirit that the western world remembers Wenceslas. Often he would take food, clothing, and fuel to the poor people of his kingdom. On Stephen the Martyr's Feast Day (December 26 in the Western Church and December 27 in the Eastern Church), Wenceslas would usually be seen tramping through the woods laden with fowl, bread, and other foods from his own table. He would distribute these gifts to the starving and poor. A young page might also be observed following in his footsteps with firewood and other items to give to the less fortunate. In the 1800s, a mission worker named John Neale wrote a Christmas carol about Wenceslas. The words of "Good King Wenceslas" beautifully tell the story of the kindhearted duke.

Although Wenceslas was kind and good, he had many enemies. Those who still clung to the pagan religion resented his Christian influence on the country. Wenceslas also agreed to pay tribute to King Henry I of Germany rather than have Bohemia invaded by the Germans. Political unrest between the Christians and pagans was like a time bomb waiting to go off.

Even during the tension, Wenceslas still maintained his generous spirit. Sometime during the 920s, he was married and had a son. Boleslav also married and had a son. To celebrate the event, Boleslav invited Wenceslas to his castle, where he was still in exile. Despite warnings of treachery, Wenceslas accepted. After a great feast Wenceslas made his way to the chapel, just as he did every night. Unsuspecting, he went alone. At the door of the chapel, several of Boleslav's associates attacked Wenceslas, and then the cruel brother himself appeared and lunged a lance into the duke's body. With his last breath Wenceslas said, "May God forgive you, brother."

The death of Wenceslas brought about intense mourning among the Christians of Bohemia. The exact date of his death is unknown; it might have been in 929, 935, or 938. With Wenceslas out of the way, Boleslav became the ruler of Bohemia and was known as Boleslav the Cruel. After Boleslav's death, the baby whose birth had brought Wenceslas to Stara-Boleslav became the national leader. He took after his uncle in virtue and benevolence and was called Boleslav the Pious.

Wenceslas is associated with Christmas because of the carol and also because of his kind gift giving at this time of year. It is thought that he may even be the inspiration (along with St. Nicholas) for our Santa Claus. This tenth-century ruler has been memorialized in legend and true history. His native country has made him their patron saint. Truly, his life is an example of Christian charity and one which should be imitated.

A Christmas Greeting

A Merry Christmas morning
To each and every one!
The rose has kissed the dawning
And the gold is in the sun.

And may the Christmas splendor
A joyous greeting bear,
Of love that's true and tender
And faith that's sweet and fair!
~Unknown

Good King Wenceslas
By John Mason Neale

Good King Wenceslas looked out,
On the Feast of Stephen,
When the snow lay round about,
Deep, and crisp, and even:

Brightly shone the moon that night,
Though the frost was cruel,
When a poor man came in sight,
Gath'ring winter fuel.

"Hither, page, and stand by me,
If thou know'st it, telling,
Yonder peasant, who is he?
Where and what his dwelling?"

"Sire, he lives a good league hence,
Underneath the mountain;
Right against the forest fence,
By St. Agnes' fountain."

"Bring me flesh, and bring me wine,
Bring me pine logs hither;
Thou and I will see him dine,
When we bear them thither."

Page and monarch forth they went,
Forth they went together;
Through the rude wind's wild lament,
And the bitter weather.

"Sire, the night is darker now,
And the wind blows stronger;
Fails my heart, I know not how,
I can go no longer."

"Mark my footsteps, good my page!
Tread thou in them boldly;
Thou shalt find the winter's rage
Freeze thy blood less coldly."

In his master's steps he trod,
Where the snow lay dinted;
Heat was in the very sod
Which the saint had printed.

Therefore, Christian men, be sure,
Wealth or rank possessing,
Ye who now will bless the poor,
Shall yourselves find blessing.

Christmas Cooking

Fudge

2 cup sugar
½ cup water
½ cup corn syrup
2 ounces unsweetened baking chocolate
2 tablespoons butter
1 teaspoon vanilla

Mix the sugar with the water. Add the chocolate and corn syrup. Stir over medium heat until mixed. Boil gently to a "soft ball" stage (see Tests for Syrups below). Just before removing from the stove, add the butter; then beat the mixture until it thickens. Add the vanilla, and pour into a buttered pan. Cut into squares; when cool the fudge is ready for serving.

Butterscotch

3 cups light brown sugar
¼ cup butter
¼ cup vinegar or juice of 1 lemon
½ cup water

Mix the sugar and liquids thoroughly. Boil gently to the "crack" stage (see Tests for Syrups below). Add the butter. Pour into buttered cookie sheet. When almost cool, cut into squares with a pizza cutter. Break into pieces when cold.

Tests for Syrups

(a) Thread: when dropped from a spoon, the syrup forms a thread about two inches long (230° F)
(b) Soft ball: when dropped into cold water, the syrup forms a soft ball if rolled between the fingers (236° F).
(c) Hard ball: when dropped into cold water, the syrup forms a firm ball (252° F).
(d) Crack: when dropped into cold water, the syrup becomes brittle (270° F).

Parisian Sweets

Chop equal parts of figs, dates, and nuts together. Knead on a board dredged with confectioner's sugar until well blended. Roll to 1/3 inch thickness, cut into cubes or rounds, and dip each piece in confectioner's sugar. Store in tin box.

December 10

Paulina's Christmas
A Story of Russian Life
Adapted from Anna Robinson's Little Paulina

One day, in Russia, there was a heavy snowstorm. The snow was deep on the ground; and in the forest the branches of the trees bent under its weight.

In this forest a little girl was struggling along. There was no path for her to follow, for the snow covered all the paths. The little girl's name was Paulina. She was dressed in a long fur coat, and she wore a cap and mittens and gaiters of fur, so that she looked more like a little furry animal than a little girl. She kept tramping along, not a bit afraid, when suddenly she heard a call for help.

"Help! Help!" the call came.

"Coming, coming!" she called back. She went in the direction of the voice and soon she saw a man making his way toward her. His dress was that of a peasant.

"Will you please direct me out of this forest, little one?" he asked. "You probably know the paths about."

"No, I am a stranger here," Paulina answered. "I live in Kief—that is, I did live there; but I am on my way to my father."

"Where is your father?" asked the man.

"He is in Siberia. They banished him."

"But, little one," said the stranger, "that is a terrible place for a child to go to. That frozen country, where wicked people are sent!"

"Oh, yes,—but my father is there, you know," said Paulina.

"Who is your father?" the man asked.

The little girl was about to tell him, when she noticed a look of interest on the stranger's face, so she said, "Did you say that you had lost your way in the forest? Do you live far from here?"

"Yes, very far. I am lost, and am nearly perishing from hunger and cold. How far is it to the next village?"

"They told me it was some miles on," said the child. "But I will take you back to the woodsman's cottage where I spent the night. The woman is a kind-hearted person, and I am sure she will give you shelter."

"That is kind of you, little one," said the stranger, "but you will be hindering your own journey if you do that."

"I know that my father would want me to show a kindness, even though it did put me back some," Paulina said.

"You must have a good father, to give you such training. Why did the Emperor send him into exile?" the stranger asked her.

"Oh, my father had enemies who lied to the Emperor—and there was no chance given to my father to explain. So the Emperor sent him away to Siberia,—and I am trying to find my way there to him."

While they walked through the forest, the stranger told Paulina about his own little daughter who was expecting him to spend Christmas with her. At last they reached the woodsman's hut. The woman greeted them kindly, and while Paulina went into another room to help her prepare the evening meal, the stranger was left warming himself by the fire, and rocking the cradle.

Once Paulina thought she heard voices, as if the stranger were talking to someone; but when she went back, she found him alone, still warming his hands and rocking the cradle with his foot.

That night the stranger slept on the floor in front of the fire—there was no other place for him; but he was glad to be safe from the storm outside.

Early in the morning, the two started out through the forest again. They must hurry, if they were to reach the next village before darkness fell. The storm had passed over, and the day was cold and clear, a beautiful winter's day. The little girl and the stranger reached the village on the other side of the forest early in the afternoon, and there before them they saw a beautiful sleigh drawn by four horses. There were four servants standing near.

"What a lovely sleigh!" exclaimed Paulina.

"Yes, I wonder where they are going. I will ask them," the stranger said. He went nearer the men and spoke to them.

"We are driving for our master to Igorhof," they said.

"Why, that is where my daughter is. If I might only ride with you, I could spend Christmas with her. Tomorrow is Christmas day, you know. And, little one, you could spend Christmas with us, too."

"Oh, no," said Paulina. "I could not take the time. I must hurry on to my father. But it would be lovely if we could only ride in this beautiful sleigh."

"You could spend the night with us, and then we could set you on your way, because you have been so kind to me," the man told her.

The servants were willing to let them ride in the beautiful sleigh, and soon they were speeding over the snow toward the great city. Once, the stranger took a scarf from a pocket on the side of the sleigh and threw it about his neck. Paulina frowned, and promptly placed it back in the pocket.

"It isn't right for you to touch anything in the sleigh. It belongs to someone else. I am beginning to fear that you may not be an honest man," she said gravely.

The stranger laughed at her, but he did not take the scarf again. They sped on over the snow until, as darkness fell, they reached the city. Soon they entered a large courtyard, and the stranger took Paulina's hand and led her into a narrow passageway, and up a small winding stairway.

"Where are you taking me?" asked Paulina. "I feel almost sure now, that you are not an honest man. I think that you may even be a thief!"

The man laughed again.

"No, I am an honest man. You will believe me when you see my little daughter. I trusted you in the forest. Now you trust me."

He led her into a large room, and they sat down upon a sofa.

"We will wait here until my daughter comes," he said.

Soon the door opened, and a beautiful little girl, about as large as Paulina, came toward them. She looked puzzled when she saw the rough-looking man with the little girl. She went close to the stranger and looked into his face.

"It is my father!" she cried, and threw her arms around his neck.

"But why are you dressed like a peasant? Has there been an accident? And who is this little stranger?"

The man took her on his lap and told her how his sleigh had been overturned in the storm, and how he had found his way to a peasant's hut, where they had given him dry clothes to put on, and how he had started out alone to find his way through the forest; and how he was nearly perishing with cold and hunger when this little girl had rescued him, and how, if it had not been for her, he would have died in the snow in the forest. He told her how little Paulina was on her way to Siberia to find her father, and how they went to the woodsman's hut where a servant had found him, and how he had planned for the sleigh to meet them on the other side of the forest.

"Oh," Paulina interrupted him, "then there was somebody talking with you when we were preparing the evening meal?"

"Yes, and everything came out just as I had planned. And do you know, little daughter, this Paulina would not let me put my own scarf around my neck. She thought that I was a thief. She is an honest little girl. But she will not tell me her name. She does not trust me."

"But why should I trust you, when you will not tell me who you are, or anything about yourself?" Paulina asked.

"Do trust my father, Paulina. I'm sure he can help you. He will tell you who he is soon, I know," the beautiful little girl said.

"Yes, little one," the stranger said. "I know someone who could speak to the Emperor about your father, and perhaps he could be pardoned. Please tell me your name; and then before you go away I will answer any questions about myself you may ask me."

"Do tell my father, Paulina," the little girl urged.

Paulina threw her arms about the stranger's knees.

"Oh, if you could only get the Emperor to pardon him.—But I do not ask for a pardon—he has done nothing to be pardoned for. All that I ask is that he may have justice done him. My father is Vladimir Betzkoi."

The stranger frowned, and then he whispered, "There must be some mistake. He must be a good man to have such an honest little daughter." Then he said to Paulina, "Do you believe now that I am an honest man, since you have seen my daughter?"

"Oh, yes, indeed I do. You couldn't help being good and honest. She is so beautiful. I think her face is like what a queen's should be," Paulina answered eagerly.

The stranger and his little daughter smiled, and the man said, "Well, I believe that your father is an honest man since I have seen you. And I can tell you now, I know he will be pardoned."

"Tell her, father, tell the little Paulina who you are," his daughter whispered.

"Until your father returns to you, little one, you must stay here and I will be a father to you—as I am father to all the people of Russia, for I am the Emperor!"

Just then the bells began ringing, and voices outside began singing,—for it was the beginning of Christmas morning. And Paulina said,

"This is the happiest Christmas morning I have ever known."

Time Flies: A Reading Diary
by Christina Rossetti

Christmas hath a darkness
Brighter than the blazing noon,
Christmas hath a chillness
Warmer than the heat of June,
Christmas hath a beauty
Lovelier than the world can show,
For Christmas bringeth Jesus
Brought for us so low.
Earth, strike up your music,
Heaven hath answering music,
For all Angels soon to sing;
Birds that sing and bells that ring;
Earth, put on your whitest
Bridal robe of spotless snow,
For Christmas bringeth Jesus
Brought for us so low.

Christmas Carols

Next 2 pages. Sing the two Christmas Carols together as a family. Discuss what the songs mean.

O Little Town of Bethlehem

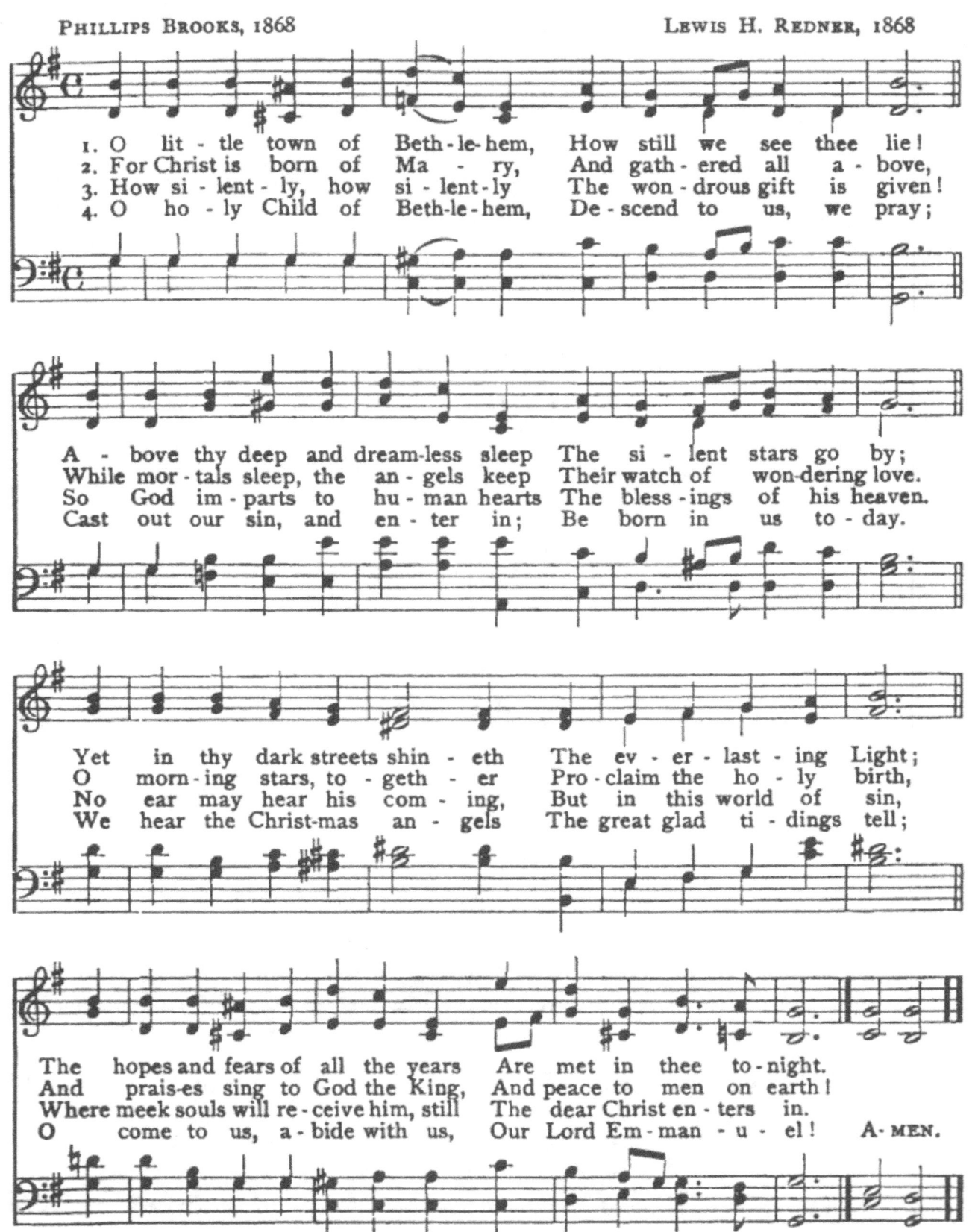

Joy to the World!

Countdown to Christmas   61   Amy Puetz Fox

December 11

Christmas Storms and Sunshine
Part 1
By Elizabeth Gaskell

In the town of —— (no matter where) there circulated two local newspapers (no matter when). Now the *Flying Post* was long established and respectable—alias bigoted and Tory; the *Examiner* was spirited and intelligent—alias new-fangled and democratic. Every week these newspapers contained articles abusing each other; as cross and peppery as articles could be, and evidently the production of irritated minds, although they seemed to have one stereotyped commencement,—"Though the article appearing in last week's *Post* (or *Examiner*) is below contempt, yet we have been induced," etc., etc., and every Saturday the Radical shopkeepers shook hands together, and agreed that the *Post* was done for, by the slashing, clever *Examiner*; while the more dignified Tories began by regretting that Johnson should think that low paper, only read by a few of the vulgar, worth wasting his wit upon; however the *Examiner* was at its last gasp.

It was not though. It lived and flourished; at least it paid its way, as one of the heroes of my story could tell. He was chief compositor, or whatever title may be given to the head man of the mechanical part of a newspaper. He hardly confined himself to that department. Once or twice, unknown to the editor, when the manuscript had fallen short, he had filled up the vacant space by compositions of his own; announcements of a forthcoming crop of green peas in December; a grey thrush having been seen, or a white hare, or such interesting phenomena; invented for the occasion, I must confess; but what of that? His wife always knew when to expect a little specimen of her husband's literary talent by a peculiar cough, which served as prelude; and, judging from this encouraging sign, and the high-pitched and emphatic voice in which he read them, she was inclined to think, that an "Ode to an early Rose-bud," in the corner devoted to original poetry, and a letter in the correspondence department, signed "Pro Bono Publico," were her husband's writing, and to hold up her head accordingly.

I never could find out what it was that occasioned the Hodgsons to lodge in the same house as the Jenkinses. Jenkins held the same office in the Tory paper as Hodgson did in the *Examiner*, and, as I said before, I leave you to give it a name. But Jenkins had a proper sense of his position, and a proper reverence for all in authority, from the king down to the editor and sub-editor. He would as soon have thought of borrowing the king's crown for a nightcap, or the king's scepter for a walking-stick, as he would have thought of filling up any spare corner with any production of his own; and I think it would have even added to his contempt of Hodgson (if that were possible), had he known of the "productions of his brain," as the latter fondly alluded to the paragraphs he inserted, when speaking to his wife.

Jenkins had his wife too. Wives were wanting to finish the completeness of the quarrel, which existed one memorable Christmas week, some dozen years ago, between the two neighbors, the two compositors. And with wives, it was a very pretty, a very complete quarrel. To make the opposing parties still more equal, still more well-matched, if the Hodgsons had a baby ("such a baby!—a poor, puny little thing"), Mrs. Jenkins had a cat ("such a cat! a great, nasty, meowing tom-cat, that was always stealing the milk put by for little Angel's supper"). And now, having matched Greek with Greek, I must proceed to the tug of war. It was the day before Christmas; such a cold east wind! Such an inky sky! Such a blue-black look in people's faces, as they were driven out more than usual, to complete their purchases for the next day's festival.

Before leaving home that morning, Jenkins had given some money to his wife to buy the next day's dinner.

"My dear, I wish for turkey and sausages. It may be a weakness, but I own I am partial to sausages. My deceased mother was. Such tastes are hereditary. As to the sweets—whether plum-pudding or mince-pies—I leave such considerations to you; I only beg you not to mind expense. Christmas comes but once a year."

And again he had called out from the bottom of the first flight of stairs, just close to the Hodgsons' door ("such ostentatiousness," as

Mrs. Hodgson observed), "You will not forget the sausages, my dear?"

"I should have liked to have had something above common, Mary," said Hodgson, as they too made their plans for the next day, "but I think roast beef must do for us. You see, love, we've a family."

"Only one, Jem! I don't want more than roast beef though, I'm sure. Before I went to service, mother and me would have thought roast beef a very fine dinner."

"Well, let's settle it then, roast beef and a plum-pudding; and now, good-by. Mind and take care of little Tom. I thought he was a bit hoarse this morning."

And off he went to his work.

Now, it was a good while since Mrs. Jenkins and Mrs. Hodgson had spoken to each other, although they were quite as much in possession of the knowledge of events and opinions as though they did. Mary knew that Mrs. Jenkins despised her for not having a real lace cap, which Mrs. Jenkins had; and for having been a servant, which Mrs. Jenkins had not; and the little occasional pinchings which the Hodgsons were obliged to resort to, to make both ends meet, would have been very patiently endured by Mary, if she had not winced under Mrs. Jenkins's knowledge of such economy. But she had her revenge. She had a child, and Mrs. Jenkins had none. To have had a child, even such a puny baby as little Tom, Mrs. Jenkins would have worn commonest caps, and cleaned grates, and drudged her fingers to the bone. The great unspoken disappointment of her life soured her temper, and turned her thoughts inward, and made her morbid and selfish.

"Hang that cat! He's been stealing again! He's gnawed the cold mutton in his nasty mouth till it's not fit to set before a Christian; and I've nothing else for Jem's dinner. But I'll give it him now I've caught him, that I will!"

So saying, Mary Hodgson caught up her husband's Sunday cane, and despite the cat's cries and scratches, she gave him such a beating as she hoped might cure him of his thievish propensities; when lo! and behold, Mrs. Jenkins stood at the door with a face of bitter wrath.

"Aren't you ashamed of yourself ma'am, to abuse a poor dumb animal, ma'am, as knows no better than to take food when he sees it, ma'am? He only follows the nature which God has given, ma'am; and it's a pity your nature, ma'am, which I've heard, is of the stingy saving species, does not make you shut your cupboard door a little closer. There is such a thing as law for brute animals. I'll ask Mr. Jenkins, but I don't think them Radicals has done away with that law yet, for all their Reform Bill, ma'am. My poor precious love of a Tommy, is he hurt? And is his leg broke for taking a mouthful of scraps, as most people would give away to a beggar,—if he'd take 'em?" wound up Mrs. Jenkins, casting a contemptuous look on the remnant of a scrag end of mutton.

Mary felt very angry and very guilty. For she really pitied the poor limping animal as he crept up to his mistress, and there lay down to bemoan himself; she wished she had not beaten him so hard, for it certainly was her own careless way of never shutting the cupboard door that had tempted him to his fault. But the sneer at her little bit of mutton turned her penitence to fresh wrath, and she shut the door in Mrs. Jenkins's face, as she stood caressing her cat in the lobby, with such a bang, that it wakened little Tom, and he began to cry.

Everything was to go wrong with Mary today. Now baby was awake, who was to take her husband's dinner to the office? She took the child in her arms, and tried to hush him off to sleep again, and as she sung she cried, she could hardly tell why,—a sort of reaction from her violent angry feelings. She wished she had never beaten the poor cat; she wondered if his leg was really broken. What would her mother say if she knew how cross and cruel her little Mary was getting? If she should live to beat her child in one of her angry fits?

It was of no use lullabying while she sobbed so; it must be given up, and she must just carry her baby in her arms, and take him with her to the office, for it was long past dinner time. So she pared the mutton carefully, although by so doing she reduced the meat to an infinitesimal quantity, and taking the baked potatoes out of the oven, she popped them piping hot into her basket with the addition of plate, butter, salt, and knife and fork.

It was, indeed, a bitter wind. She bent against it as she ran, and the flakes of snow were sharp and cutting as ice. Baby cried all the way, though she cuddled him up in her shawl. Then her husband had made his appetite up for a potato pie, and (literary man as he was) his body got so much the better of his mind, that he looked rather black at the cold mutton. Mary had no appetite for her own dinner when she arrived at home again. So, after she had tried to feed baby, and he had fretfully refused to take his bread and milk, she laid him down as usual on his quilt, surrounded by play things, while she sided away, and chopped suet for the next day's pudding. Early in the afternoon a parcel came, done up first in brown paper, then in such a white, grass-bleached, sweet-smelling towel, and a note from her dear, dear mother; in which quaint writing she endeavored to tell her daughter that she was not forgotten at Christmas time; but that learning that Farmer Burton was killing his pig, she had made interest for some of his famous pork, out of which she had manufactured some sausages, and flavored them just as Mary used to like when she lived at home.

"Dear, dear mother!" said Mary to herself. "There never was anyone like her for remembering other folk. What rare sausages she used to make! Home things have a smack with 'em, no bought things can ever have. Set them up with their sausages! I've a notion if Mrs. Jenkins had ever tasted mother's she'd have no fancy for them town-made things Fanny took in just now."

And so she went on thinking about home, till the smiles and the dimples came out again at the remembrance of that pretty cottage, which would look green even now in the depth of winter, with its pyracanthus, and its holly-bushes, and the great Portugal laurel that was her mother's pride. And the back path through the orchard to Farmer Burton's; how well she remembered it. The bushels of unripe apples she had picked up there, and distributed among his pigs, till he had scolded her for giving them so much green trash.

She was interrupted—her baby (I call him a baby, because his father and mother did, and because he was so little of his age, but I rather think he was eighteen months old) had fallen asleep some time before among his playthings; an uneasy, restless sleep; but of which Mary had been thankful, as his morning's nap had been too short, and as she was so busy. But now he began to make such a strange crowing noise, just like a chair drawn heavily and gratingly along a kitchen floor! His eyes were open, but expressive of nothing but pain.

"Mother's darling!" said Mary, in terror, lifting him up. "Baby, try not to make that noise. Hush, hush, darling; what hurts him?" But the noise came worse and worse.

"Fanny! Fanny!" Mary called in mortal fright, for her baby was almost black with his gasping breath, and she had no one to ask for aid or sympathy but her landlady's daughter, a little girl of twelve or thirteen, who attended to the house in her mother's absence, as daily cook in gentlemen's families. Fanny was more especially considered the attendant of the upstairs lodgers (who paid for the use of the kitchen, "for Jenkins could not abide the smell of meat cooking"), but just now she was fortunately sitting at her afternoon's work of darning stockings, and hearing Mrs. Hodgson's cry of terror, she ran to her sitting room, and understood the case at a glance.

"He's got the croup! Oh, Mrs. Hodgson, he'll die as sure as fate. Little brother had it, and he died in no time. The doctor said he could do nothing for him—it had gone too far. He said if we'd put him in a warm bath at first, it might have saved him; but, bless you! He was never half so bad as your baby." Unconsciously there mingled in her statement some of a child's love of producing an effect; but the increasing danger was clear enough.

"Oh, my baby! My baby! Oh, love, love! Don't look so ill; I cannot bear it. And my fire so low! There, I was thinking of home, and picking currants, and never minding the fire. Oh, Fanny! What is the fire like in the kitchen? Speak."

"Mother told me to screw it up, and throw some slack on as soon as Mrs. Jenkins had done with it, and so I did. It's very low and black. But, oh, Mrs. Hodgson! Let me run for the doctor—I cannot bear to hear him, it's so like little brother."

Through her streaming tears Mary motioned her to go; and trembling, sinking, sick at heart, she laid her boy in his cradle, and ran to fill her kettle.

To be continued . . .

A Christmas Carol
By Christina Rossetti

*In the bleak mid-winter
Frosty wind made moan,
Earth stood hard as iron,
Water like a stone;
Snow had fallen, snow on snow,
Snow on snow,
In the bleak mid-winter
Long ago.*

*Our God, Heaven cannot hold Him
Nor earth sustain;
Heaven and earth shall flee away
When He comes to reign:
In the bleak mid-winter
A stable-place sufficed
The Lord God Almighty
Jesus Christ.*

*Enough for Him whom cherubim
Worship night and day,
A breastful of milk
And a mangerful of hay;*

*Enough for Him whom angels
Fall down before,
The ox and ass and camel
Which adore.*

*Angels and archangels
May have gathered there,
Cherubim and seraphim
Throng'd the air,
But only His mother
In her maiden bliss
Worshipped her Beloved
With a kiss.*

*What can I give Him,
Poor as I am?
If I were a shepherd
I would bring a lamb,
If I were a wise man
I would do my part,—
Yet what I can I give Him,
Give my heart.*

Christmas Play

"We could put the two big dolls behind a blanket. Then when it's time for the three wise men scene all we have to do is move the blanket and the dolls can be Mary and Joseph," I suggested to my two sisters.

"Yeah, that would work," Sarah agreed, "and we can use the other doll for Mary when she is on the donkey."

All these preparations for our annual Christmas production took place many years ago. My sisters and I would create a script and then begin practicing. It did take some imagination because there were only three of us and we were all girls! In the final production, I ended up being the donkey with Mary (a doll) on my back. My younger sister, Marissa, was Joseph in the first scene; and Sarah, the oldest, was the mean inn keeper with NO ROOM. Then in the next scene, two of us were shepherds watching over our flock at night, and the third sister appeared as the angel. Each year we had to alternate who got to play the role of the angel because we all loved to play that part. Next we would appear as the three wise men, singing the song and carrying pretend gold, frankincense, and myrrh. The script was fairly easy to write because we just recited the story from the Bible, usually from the King James Version because it sounded more poetic: "And it came to pass in those days, that there went out a decree from Caesar Augustus. . . ." To keep the story moving along, we added Christmas carols for each scene. The angel sang "Hark! The Herald Angels Sing," the shepherds sang "Silent Night," and the manger scene was accompanied by "What Child is This?" or "Away in a Manger." Our finale was always "Jingle Bells." We preformed the play on Christmas Eve for our parents.

For today's activity, why don't you begin creating your own Christmas play? You could do the story of Jesus' birth just like my sisters and I used to, or you could write your own play, or you could use some of the stories from this book to make a play. (The only exceptions are the stories on December 9 and 13.)

My personal favorite is "Becky's Christmas Dream," and I can imagine if my sisters and I were still children that we would have created a play from that story. Here is how we would have done it. First we would have decided who would get which part. Since Marissa was the youngest she would have been Becky. I would probably have been the cat. For a costume I would have worn a belt tied to my shirt for a tail and had some ears attached to a headband. Sarah would have been given the role of the clock. Simply holding a clock face over her own would have sufficed for a costume. Then she would have come back into the room as a tea kettle. Anyone can be a kettle—simply extend one hand for the spout and put the other on your hip for a handle. For the next scene we would have been the family in the sleigh talking about Becky. Some of the parts would have been eliminated, but mother and Aunt Sally would have been played by Sarah and me. In the finale, we would have come in on the sleeping Becky (Marissa).

Now it is your turn. How could you create a play from "Why the Chimes Rang" or "The Fir-Tree?" The play could be performed by the children for the parents or the whole family could take part and perform the play for grandparents, aunts, uncles, and cousins. Use your imagination and make sure you have fun. Another idea is to have everyone either sing a song, or recite a poem or Bible verse. This could be done on Christmas Eve or Christmas day and include every member of the family. Whatever you decide to do, set aside a little time every day or every other day between now and Christmas to practice.

December 12

Christmas Storms and Sunshine
Part 2
By Elizabeth Gaskell

Mrs. Jenkins, having cooked her husband's snug little dinner, to which he came home; having told him her story of the cat's beating, at which he was justly and dignifiedly, indignant, saying it was all of a piece with that abusive Examiner; having received the sausages, and turkey, and mince pies, which her husband had ordered; and cleaned up the room, and prepared everything for tea, and coaxed and duly bemoaned her cat (who had pretty nearly forgotten his beating, but very much enjoyed the petting), having done all these and many other things, Mrs. Jenkins sat down to get up the real lace cap. Every thread was pulled out separately, and carefully stretched: when, what was that? Outside, in the street, a chorus of piping children's voices sang the old carol she had heard a hundred times in the days of her youth:—

"As Joseph was a walking he heard an angel sing,
'This night shall be born our heavenly King.
He neither shall be born in housen nor in hall,
Nor in the place of Paradise, but in an ox's stall.
He neither shall be clothed in purple nor in pall,
But all in fair linen, as were babies all:
He neither shall be rocked in silver nor in gold,
But in a wooden cradle that rocks on the mould," etc.

She got up and went to the window. There, below, stood the group of black little figures, relieved against the snow, which now enveloped everything. "For old sake's sake," as she phrased it, she counted out a halfpenny apiece for the singers, out of the copper bag, and threw them down below.

The room had become chilly while she had been counting out and throwing down her money, so she stirred her already glowing fire, and sat down right before it—but not to stretch her lace; like Mary Hodgson, she began to think over long-past days, on softening remembrances of the dead and gone, on words long forgotten, on holy stories heard at her mother's knee.

"I cannot think what's come over me tonight," said she, half aloud, recovering herself by the sound of her own voice from her train of thought—"My head goes wandering on them old times. I'm sure more texts have come into my head with thinking on my mother within this last half hour, than I've thought on for years and years. I hope I'm not going to die. Folks say, thinking too much on the dead betokens we're going to join 'em; I should be loth to go just yet—such a fine turkey as we've got for dinner tomorrow, too!"

Knock, knock, knock, at the door, as fast as knuckles could go. And then, as if the comer could not wait, the door was opened, and Mary Hodgson stood there as white as death.

"Mrs. Jenkins! Oh, your kettle is boiling, thank God! Let me have the water for my baby, for the love of God! He's got croup, and is dying!"

Mrs. Jenkins turned on her chair with a wooden inflexible look on her face, that (between ourselves) her husband knew and dreaded for all his pompous dignity.

"I'm sorry I can't oblige you, ma'am; my kettle is wanted for my husband's tea. Don't be afeared, Tommy, Mrs. Hodgson won't venture to intrude herself where she's not desired. You'd better send for the doctor, ma'am, instead of wasting your time in wringing your hands, ma'am—my kettle is engaged."

Mary clasped her hands together with passionate force, but spoke no word of entreaty to that wooden face—that sharp, determined voice; but, as she turned away, she prayed for strength to bear the coming trial, and strength to forgive Mrs. Jenkins.

Mrs. Jenkins watched her go away meekly, as one who has no hope, and then she turned upon herself as sharply as she ever did on anyone else.

"What a brute I am, Lord forgive me! What's my husband's tea to a baby's life? In croup, too, where time is everything. You crabbed old vixen, you! Anyone may know you never had a child!"

She was downstairs (kettle in hand) before she had finished her self-upbraiding; and when in Mrs. Hodgson's room, she rejected all thanks (Mary had not the voice for many words), saying, stiffly, "I do it for the poor baby's sake, ma'am, hoping he may live to have mercy to poor dumb beasts, if he does forget to lock his cupboards."

But she did everything, and more than Mary, with her young inexperience, could have thought of. She prepared the warm bath, and tried it with her husband's own thermometer (Mr. Jenkins was as punctual as clockwork in noting down the temperature of every day). She let his mother place her baby in the tub, still preserving the same rigid, affronted aspect, and then she went upstairs without a word. Mary longed to ask her to stay, but dared not; though, when she left the room, the tears chased each other down her cheeks faster than ever. Poor young mother, how she counted the minutes till the doctor should come. But, before he came, down again stalked Mrs. Jenkins, with something in her hand.

"I've seen many of these croup-fits, which, I take it, you've not, ma'am. Mustard plasters is very sovereign, put on the throat; I've been up and made one, ma'am, and, by your leave, I'll put it on the poor little fellow."

Mary could not speak, but she signed her grateful assent.

It began to smart while they still kept silence; and he looked up to his mother as if seeking courage from her looks to bear the stinging pain; but she was softly crying, to see him suffer, and her want of courage reacted upon him, and he began to sob aloud. Instantly Mrs. Jenkins's apron was up, hiding her face: "Peep-bo, baby," said she, as merrily as she could. His little face brightened, and his mother having once got the cue, the two women kept the little fellow amused, until his plaster had taken effect.

"He's better—oh, Mrs. Jenkins, look at his eyes! How different! And he breathes quite softly."

As Mary spoke thus, the doctor entered. He examined his patient. Baby was really better.

"It has been a sharp attack, but the remedies you have applied have been worth all the Pharmacopoeia an hour later—I shall send a powder," etc. etc.

Mrs. Jenkins stayed to hear this opinion; and (her heart wonderfully more easy) was going to leave the room, when Mary seized her hand and kissed it; she could not speak her gratitude. Mrs. Jenkins looked affronted and awkward, and as if she must go upstairs and wash her hand directly.

But, in spite of these sour looks, she came softly down an hour or so afterwards to see how baby was.

The little gentleman slept well after the fright he had given his friends; and on Christmas morning, when Mary awoke and looked at the sweet little pale face lying on her arm, she could hardly realize the danger he had been in.

When she came down (later than usual), she found the household in a commotion. What do you think had happened? Why, the cat had been a traitor to his best friend, and eaten up some of Mr. Jenkins's own special sausages; and gnawed and tumbled the rest so, that they were not fit to be eaten! There were no bounds to that cat's appetite! He would have eaten his own father if he had been tender enough. And now Mrs. Jenkins stormed and cried—"Hang the cat!"

Christmas Day, too! And all the shops shut! "What was turkey without sausages?" gruffly asked Mr. Jenkins.

"Oh, Jem!" whispered Mary, "hearken what a piece of work he's making about sausages—I should like to take Mrs. Jenkins up some of mother's; they're twice as good as bought sausages."

"I see no objection, my dear. Sausages do not involve intimacies, else his politics are what I can no ways respect."

"But, oh, Jem, if you had seen her last night about baby! I'm sure she may scold me forever, and I'll not answer. I'd even make her cat welcome to the sausages." The tears gathered to Mary's eyes as she kissed her boy.

"Better take 'em upstairs, my dear, and give them to the cat's mistress." And Jem chuckled at his saying.

Mary put them on a plate, but still she loitered.

"What must I say, Jem? I never know."

"Say—I hope you'll accept of these sausages, as my mother—no, that's not grammar,—say what comes uppermost, Mary, it will be sure to be right."

So Mary carried them upstairs and knocked at the door; and when told to "come in," she looked very red, but went up to Mrs. Jenkins, saying, "Please take these. Mother made them." And was away before an answer could be given.

Just as Hodgson was ready to go to church, Mrs. Jenkins came downstairs, and called Fanny. In a minute, the latter entered the Hodgsons' room, and delivered Mr. and Mrs. Jenkins's compliments and they would be particular glad if Mr. and Mrs. Hodgson would eat their dinner with them.

"And carry baby upstairs in a shawl, be sure," added Mrs. Jenkins's voice in the passage, close to the door, whither she had followed her messenger. There was no discussing the matter, with the certainty of every word being overheard.

Mary looked anxiously at her husband. She remembered his saying he did not approve of Mr. Jenkins's politics.

"Do you think it would do for baby?" asked he.

"Oh, yes," answered she, eagerly; "I would wrap him up so warm."

"And I've got our room up to sixty-five already, for all it's so frosty," added the voice outside.

Now, how do you think they settled the matter? The very best way in the world. Mr. and Mrs. Jenkins came down into the Hodgsons' room, and dined there. Turkey at the top, roast beef at the bottom, sausages at one side, potatoes at the other. Second course, plum-pudding at the top, and mince pies at the bottom.

And after dinner, Mrs. Jenkins would have baby on her knee and he seemed quite to take to her; she declared he was admiring the real lace on her cap, but Mary thought (though she did not say so) that he was pleased by her kind looks and coaxing words. Then he was wrapped up and carried carefully upstairs to tea, in Mrs. Jenkins's room. And after tea, Mrs. Jenkins, and Mary, and her husband, found out each other's mutual liking for music, and sat singing old glees and catches, till I don't know what o'clock, without one word of politics or newspapers.

Before they parted, Mary had coaxed kitty on to her knee; for Mrs. Jenkins would not part with baby, who was sleeping on her lap.

"When you're busy, bring him to me. Do, now, it will be a real favor. I know you must have a deal to do, with another coming; let him come up to me. I'll take the greatest of cares of him; pretty darling, how sweet he looks when he's asleep!"

When the couples were once more alone, the husbands unburdened their minds to their wives.

Mr. Jenkins said to his—"Do you know, Burgess tried to make me believe Hodgson was such a fool as to put paragraphs into the Examiner now and then; but I see he knows his place, and has got too much sense to do any such thing."

Hodgson said—"Mary, love, I almost fancy from Jenkins's way of speaking (so much civiler than I expected), he guesses I wrote that 'Pro Bono' and the 'Rose-bud,'—at any rate, I've no objection to your naming it, if the subject should come uppermost; I should like him to know I'm a literary man."

Well! I've ended my tale; I hope you don't think it too long; but, before I go, just let me say one thing.

If any of you have any quarrels, or misunderstandings, or coolnesses, or cold shoulders, or shynesses, or tiffs, or miffs, or huffs, with anyone else, just make friends before Christmas—you will be so much merrier if you do.

I ask it of you for the sake of that old angelic song, heard so many years ago by the shepherds, keeping watch by night, on Bethlehem Heights.

The Word "Christmas" It's Orthography and Meaning
By William Francis Dawson

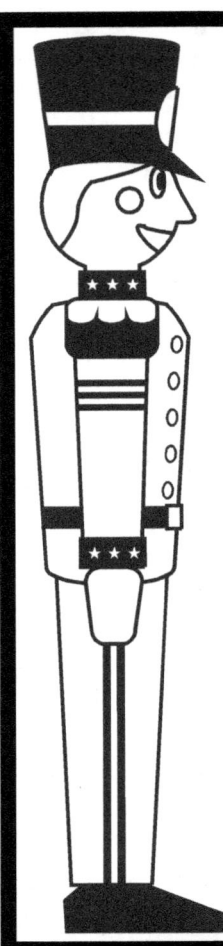

"Christmas" (pronounced Kris'mas) signifies "Christ's Mass," meaning the festival of the Nativity of Christ, and the word has been variously spelt at different periods. The following are obsolete forms of it found in old English writings: Crystmasse, Cristmes, Cristmas, Crestenmes, Crestenmas, Cristemes, Cristynmes, Crismas, Kyrsomas, Xtemas, Cristesmesse, Cristemasse, Crystenmas, Crystynmas, Chrystmas, Chrystemes, Chrystemasse, Chrystymesse, Cristenmas, Christenmas, Christmass, Christmes.

Christmas has also been called Noel or Nowel. As to the derivation of the word Noel, some say it is a contraction of the French nouvelles (tidings), les bonnes nouvelles, that is "The good news of the Gospel"; others take it as an abbreviation of the Gascon or Provencal nadaue, nadal, which means the same as the Latin natalis, that is, dies natalis, "the birthday." In "The Franklin's Tale," Chaucer alludes to "Nowel" as a festive cry at Christmastide: "And 'Nowel' crieth every lusty man." Some say Noel is a corruption of Yule, Jule, or Ule, meaning "The festival of the sun." The name Yule is still applied to the festival in Scotland, and some other places. Christmas is represented in Welsh by Nadolig, which signifies "the natal, or birth"; in French by Noel; and in Italian by Il Natale, which, together with its cognate term in Spanish, is simply a contraction of dies natalis, "the birthday."

Christmas Games

Puss in the Corner by Laura Valentine

Laura Ingalls Wilder mentions this game in her book, On the Banks of Plum Creek. In the story, Pa goes to town just before Christmas and is caught in a blizzard. Ma, Laura, and her sisters played many games to keep them from worrying. ~Amy

A boy or girl is placed at each corner of the room. One player stands in the middle as the cat. He or she goes to each kitten in the corners in turn and says, "Puss, puss, will you give me a little water?" The kitten addressed declines doing so, but meantime, while they are talking, the other kittens are beckoning to each other to change places, and, suddenly, run rapidly across to change places. The cat in the middle must be on the watch to get into one of these places. If the cat can gain a corner before one of the kittens does, he or she remains in it, and the disappointed player has to be "cat" instead.

Earth, Air, Fire, and Water
By Laura Valentine

For this game the players sit round and one stands in the midst of them, holding a handkerchief twisted into a ball. He or she counts one, two, three, and then throws the handkerchief-ball into the lap of any one he or she chooses, crying at the same time, "Earth," "Air," "Fire," or "Water," as she pleases. If she cries, "Earth," the person into whose lap the ball falls must reply instantly by naming some animal living on the earth; if the word was "Water," some fish must be named; if "Fire," something that can exist in fire; if "Air," some bird or insect. If she hesitates so long as to allow the ball-thrower to count to three, she pays a forfeit.

Example:

Edith stands in the midst of a merry group with her handkerchief ready.

Edith: One, two, three—EARTH.

Ada (into whose lap the ball falls): A lion.

Edith takes back the ball and pauses—one, two, three—then throws it at Jessy, crying, "FIRE."

Poor Jessy, very much startled, says, hurriedly, "Coals."

Edith laughs, and replies, "Oh, Jessy, coals are not animals! Pay a forfeit."

Ada: But, Edith, I think really Jessy is right. The game says, "anything that exists in the fire;" no animal can.

Edith: No, it cannot; but coals get burned up. I think, too, we might say ashes, a stuff which fire does not consume.

Edith: Well, I will let Jessy off his forfeit, as it is so difficult. Now, prepare; I am going to throw the ball again. One, two, three—AIR.

Mary (catching it): An eagle.

Edith: Very well; give me back the ball. Now, one, two, three—WATER.

Ada (hurriedly): Fish!

Edith: No, that will not do; you must name some fish.

Ada: Salmon.

Thus the game goes on. Sometimes a little player has to pay a forfeit for hesitation and slowness in answering; sometimes for naming a wrong creature as living in the element named. It is by no means easy to mention a resident in earth, air, fire, or water instantaneously with receiving the ball.

December 13

Christmas Far From Home
Based on a True Story
By Amy Puetz Fox

A lone soldier in army green sat on his cot composing a letter. Around him was the hustle and bustle of army life in the paratroop unit. He seemed to be very intent on the paper before him and almost lost in another world.

"Mac!" a burly friend called. "Say Mac, me and Dalton are gonna use our pass to visit London, you wanta come?"

Johnny McKinney, nicknamed Mac by his army buddies, looked up from his letter and replied in his slow Southern accent, "Sure! Let me finish this letter and I'll be ready."

The three friends stepped off the train wearing their dress uniforms. On each of their jackets was pinned the silver wings of the paratroopers. The year was 1943, and despite the war, the shops showed a wonderful world of Christmas cheer. It was the third Christmas since the United States had been bombed by the Japanese. So much had changed in those years and victory seemed very far away. Not that any self-respecting soldier would ever admit that they doubted victory, but still, it seemed that the "little" war should have been won long ago. All the soldiers knew they were stationed in England awaiting the word to invade Europe, but when the invasion would take place, and where, no one knew for sure.

The soldiers' lives ran into a monotonous routine of drills and training, but the three soldiers who were walking merrily along the packed streets were thinking only of Christmas and the freedom they had during their few hours of leave.

"Mac old pal, were you writing to that pretty gal of yours back home?" the rather vocal George O'Bryan asked.

Sparkling with amusement, Johnny's light blue eyes flashed. "Actually I was writing Mom. She is pregnant with her tenth child and I told her I thought the name Margie was nice. If it's a girl I suggest she could name her that." O'Bryan was visibly disappointed that he couldn't rib Mac about his sweetheart.

But O'Bryan soon thought of something else to tease him about. "Who's Margie? I thought your gal's name was Wanda, or something like that."

"Her name is Wanda! Five foot two and eyes of blue," John said with evident pride as he quoted from a popular song. "I just think Margie is a nice name." John replied with a satisfaction that O'Bryan had been unsuccessful again. The mention of Wanda brought back more recollections. He wished she were here. What good times they could have in England together, but she was in Evansville, Indiana, attending nursing school. When would he see her again?

The third member of the party, Jim Dalton, broke into his thoughts. "Look there's a JOIN THE ROYAL NAVY sign. It's too bad we don't have a camera. Remember back in the States when we were given our first pass at Fort Benning and we took such swell pictures joking about the marine and the navy draft posters?" The other two laughed at the recollection. The pictures had turned out hilarious, with them gathering around the signs in humorous expressions of dislike for any branch of the service besides the army! But they did not have a camera and so they moved on and enjoyed looking in the shop windows.

John wished he could buy a Christmas present for his folks. The very thought sent a wave of homesickness over him. How were his parents and brothers and sisters? Such a tight bond existed between the family that was forged through the long and hard years of the Depression. He wished they could be together during this festive time of year. Perhaps it was the season or the store that was playing, "I'll be Home for Christmas," or maybe it was the letter from home he'd received that morning. Whatever the reason, John began thinking of home. He remembered Pop, the strong silent Pop, who was the rock that everyone leaned on.

Right - John McKinney

No matter how badly things were they always knew that Pop would provide for them with the last breath of his being. If Pop was the rock then Mom was the song of the home. She held the tattered band together with optimism and love. No situation was so bad that she could not find a reason to laugh. Her soothing voice of optimism filled many a hungry belly. Winter was always the worst time for the poor sharecroppers in Kentucky. A pair of snow boots in a window reminded John how he and his father used to tie burlap sacks around their feet in the winter to give them traction as they went rabbit hunting with the dogs. John would knock the rabbits on the head with a stick after the dogs had found them and they would have rabbit for supper.

Left - John McKinney

"What's the matter Mac, leave your heart in Indiana?" O'Bryan jabbed John in the ribs. John had been so lost in his revelry that he hadn't heard O'Bryan talking and O'Bryan had figured that John must have been thinking about Wanda. Before John could make a reply he was seized with an asthma attack. It was as if he some invisible hand was choking the breath out of him. He doubled over while a terrible wheezing noise escaped his lips. Standing up he tried to breath deeply. This was not uncommon; John had asthma and had already been in the army hospital with pneumonia. Dalton and O'Bryan forgot what they were talking about before and commented on his problem, "Mac, how did you ever pass your physical to come to England?" O'Bryan asked after the fit had passed.

"Can't you see us being dropped behind enemy lines," Dalton injected before John answered, "and just when we come upon a nest of Nazis ol' Mac here'll have an asthma attack and spoil the whole game."

"Well, I'll tell you this much boys," John smirked, "it wasn't easy to convince the doctor to pass me, but I finally got him to see that this war couldn't possibly be won without my help." His buddies laughed as he intended, but John never really did explain how he convinced a knowledgeable doctor to sign his papers saying he was physically fit when he certainly wasn't. John had been sickly since childhood and the wet and cold of England didn't help his asthma. "Besides, Hitler really gets under my skin," he added expressing his usual saying of annoyance, "and I just figured someone had to come along to take him down."

To imagine the slight built 5'7" John taking on Hitler really was hilarious and so they all three laughed at the joke.

"You may be a crack shot Mac, but there is more to being a soldier that handling a gun," O'Bryan pointed out because he didn't have any skill with a fire arm.

"Bravery for instance?" Johnny replied. His mischief was really coming out now. Despite his build, John certainly wasn't lacking in bravery.

"You better leave the hard fighting to us burly types," O'Bryan boasted.

Unfortunately O'Bryan forgot that John and Dalton both knew of a certain instance which O'Bryan would rather forget. During their paratroop training they were planning to do their 13th jump on Friday the 13th in March of 1943, and O'Bryan was number 13 in the lineup. As they were hooked up to the cable awaiting the word to jump, O'Bryan was so worried about his number and the date that he was talking like a man about to face a firing squad. Finally John, who was number 12, offered to trade places with him. Whenever the story was mentioned afterwards O'Bryan would always jump in at this point. "And do you know where Mac landed? In a graveyard!" as if that was the worst possible fate any paratrooper could face. "A GRAVEYARD!" he would reiterate with the air of one who had been saved from the grip of death. Had John been scared? He never said, but he thought the story of his being the 13th paratrooper, on his 13th jump, on Friday the 13th and landing in a cemetery would be an interesting story to tell his children.

O'Bryan could see his friends were remembering this story so he started talking before they made a jeering comment. "Look, there is Piccadilly Square. I hear the food at the pub is swell. I'm practically starving on army food. Come on fellas, let's get a bite to eat."

The three friends agreed and in they marched ready to do battle with a couple plates of hot food! More joking and good natured teasing was also on the menu, and when they left an hour later they were really jolly.

It was still raining as John looked into a store window. Most of his army pay was gone, but he really wanted to get something pretty for Wanda this Christmas. After all Christmas was a special time of year for them because that is when they met. It had been Christmas night in 1941. He had left Kentucky at age nineteen and began driving a delivery truck for Dr. Pepper Company in Evansville, Indiana. A coworker and his girlfriend set up a blind date between him and Wanda Babb. It was love at first sight. He knew right then that someday he would marry the pretty brunet with the outgoing personality and the clear blue eyes. But then the war came and he enlisted and she continued her studies as a nurse. They simply would have to wait.

"Mac, what are you thinking about?" O'Bryan demanded.

"Just thinking about home and loved ones I guess. Ya'll know that song "I'll Be Home for Christmas" really expresses how we feel at this time of year."

His two companions silently agreed and it was obvious that they too were thinking about home. Lost in their own reflections they walked on. When they were a few blocks from Piccadilly Square, air raid sirens began going off. Everybody on the street began running for the nearest subway station. Frantic women were rushing out of stores without their purchases and urgent men were helping others along. Then they heard the planes overhead and the unearthy sound of a bomb hurrying to find a target. John and his friends joined the throng heading to the subway when the bomb exploded in Piccadilly Square. The smoke of blazing buildings hid the view from them for a few seconds and when it dissipated a horrible sight greeted them. Parts of buildings were completely missing. Wounded and injured people—who only moments before were alive and well—were walking around in confusion. Others were dead. The weight of what happened hit John like a brick of lead. If they had remained in Piccadilly Square only a few minutes more would they have been among the dead? There was no time to think! The sirens were still screaming the warning and the three soldiers hastened back to their unit.

Wanda Babb

This near brush with death took all the spirit out of the lively GI's and they returned to their barracks a little older and hardened to the reality of war. That Christmas season would forever be chiseled on John's mind as the time that he could have died but was allowed to live.

Author's Note
It is amazing how a matter of minutes can change a life forever. If Johnny McKinney had died in the bombing that day I wouldn't be here and you wouldn't be reading this story. He was my granddaddy. Before the Normandy invasion he was sent back to the states because of his asthma. His mother did have a little girl and she was named Margie Nell. Of course he married his sweetheart Wanda Babb and they had two daughters. Later in life John became a minister of the gospel. All the events in this story actually happened some artistic liberties were used to create it.

Christmas Newspaper

For today's activity we are going to make a Christmas Newspaper. The next four pages have layouts you can use. This will be a four page newspaper and would be a wonderful gift for grandparents.

The most important part of any paper is the stories it contains. Since it is a Christmas paper it needs to include stories about Christmas. You might write a story about traditions at your house. It could begin, "Christmas at our House: Each year we put up the Christmas tree on . . ." and then you could share about special food you cook at Christmas, or crafts you do, or stories you read, or songs you sing. Maybe you could ask each member of the family one thing they want for Christmas and that could be included also.

Here are questions you could use to help you get started on some articles:

1. What is the happiest Christmas you have ever spent? Tell what happened on that day.
2. Of all the Christmas gifts you have received, which gave the most joy? Why?
3. What happy surprise was ever given you on Christmas?
4. What jolly joke was ever played on you or others on Christmas?
5. What pleasant surprise have you given others at that time?
6. Of all the presents you have made for others, which do you remember with the most pleasure?
7. What makes any Christmas gift most valuable?
8. How do boys and girls often show that they have forgotten the true Christmas spirit?
9. How do they show that they have caught the true Christmas spirit?

After you have all the information you need it's time to put it on the newspaper layouts on the next four pages. Make copies of the next four pages. You can write the information on the pages or you can create them on the computer.

After you have the newspaper written and printed on the layout pages, take them to a copy machine that has 11x17 sheets of paper. Place the first and the fourth sheets on the copier as in Fig. 1 and copy. Have an employee help you insert the page with pages one and four back in the copier. Then place pages two and three as in Fig. 2 and copy. Fold the sheet in half, and now you have a genuine Christmas Newspaper. Make as many copies as you need. They would look very pretty on colored paper.

December 14

Trusty's Christmas
By Carolyn Sherwin Bailey

At first Emily and Newton were not quite sure whether or not they liked living opposite the hospital. Their father had bought the land and built their big, rambling white house on the other side of the street from the hospital because it was so quiet. But the brother and sister saw the ambulance coming almost every day to the hospital and a steady stream of doctors and nurses going and coming. Glimpses inside, when the curtains were drawn from the windows, showed row upon row of white beds. There were children in the beds too, boys and girls who seemed to be of the ages of Emily and Newton—ten and twelve.

"I just can't bear to look over at the hospital, mother," Emily said one day.

"Change your spectacles, dear," her mother advised. "You have been wearing blue goggles ever since we moved into the new house here. Put on a pair of rose-colored glasses and note what a difference it will make with what you see."

Emily laughed and then told Newton what their mother had said. It did make things seem very different, though, to look at them in a rosy light. The hospital beds emptied themselves almost as fast as they were filled. Happy, well boys and girls and grown-ups left the hospital with their friends almost every day and there were so many beautiful things happening there to watch.

The flowers that were carried into the hospital made one think of gardens that bloomed all the year. At Thanksgiving time bulging packages and baskets packed to overflowing were taken in. Before Christmas every window in the hospital was pretty with a wreath of holly. Echoes of laughter and bright glimpses of greens in the convalescent ward drifted across the street. The brother and sister began to go and come from school on the hospital side of the street, for their dread of it had changed to interest.

That was how they came to get acquainted with the blind man who sold apples and oranges at the hospital gate.

"He's always smiling, even if he is blind," Emily told them at home. "He has his fruit in a tray that hangs from his shoulder by a strap and he can make change by just feeling of the money."

"You ought to see his little dog, Trusty, though," Newton exclaimed. "He's nothing but a street dog, a fox terrier, but he knows as much as a human being. He leads his master to the hospital gate in the morning, and takes him home again at night. He holds a tin pail in his teeth for the money and he never leaves his master a minute during the day to go off and play with other dogs."

The two children began to stop every day to buy fruit for their school luncheon from the blind man. They found out that his name was Billings, and, of course, they had learned the dog's name.

"He's all the family I've got," Mr. Billings explained. "I have had him for ten years now. When we get through the day's work we go home and have a fine supper together, Trusty sitting on one side of the kitchen table and I on the other. He's my eyes and my best friend, is that little dog. I don't know what I'd do without him."

It was not long before Christmas that Newton heard sounds of a dog fight as he neared home on his way from school. It made slight impression upon him until shrill yelps of pain were mingled with the barks, and above this came a man's voice calling, "Help! Help!"

Newton ran as fast as he could in the direction of the hospital. When he reached the

gate his worst fears were realized. Trusty was in the grip of a bull dog. The bull dog, his low-hung jaw watering, had attacked Trusty apparently out of spite because the smaller dog would not give up his post by the gate. Trusty, though wiry and active, was unable to stand against such a foe, and the fierce animal, as is customary, had gotten a hold and was keeping it. He had set his teeth in Trusty's leg.

Tears were running down Mr. Billings' wrinkled cheeks. "Save Trusty, save my poor little Trusty," he begged. "I can't see where he is or I could do it myself."

If Newton had stopped to consider danger, he would probably have failed, but with a stick he went at the bull like a whirlwind. The bull dog, in turn, through sheer surprise, loosened his hold and trotted off, pretty much as if he were not interested in chewing up small dogs after all.

Emily came up then, breathless, and eager to help.

"It's all right, Mr. Billings," she assured Trusty's trembling master.

It was not all right though. Moaning with the pain of a leg almost severed by laceration and fracture, the brave little dog lay in the street, a trail of blood showing on the freshly fallen snow. "We must do something with him or he'll die," Emily said to her brother.

Newton thought a second. Then using his handkerchief as a tourniquet he stopped the bleeding to some extent, and picking up the little dog in his arms, started boldly in the hospital gate.

"I'm going to take him to father's friend, Dr. Whitman," Newton said. "Maybe he can take care of him in the laboratory where they have the monkeys and frogs. Anyway, I'll ask him."

Emily, stifling the sob that choked her as she saw Trusty lay his head on Newton's shoulder and shut his faithful brown eyes, went over to the blind man. She picked up the several apples and oranges which had fallen from his tray in the excitement and put a friendly little hand in his.

"My brother is taking your little dog into the hospital," she said. "Don't worry about him, and just stay here for the rest of the day. Newton and I will take you home tonight and we will start for school early enough in the morning to get you and bring you here. We'll do that every day and take you home until we know how Trusty is coming out."

Inside the hospital a group of half-amused nurses and two or three young physicians surrounded Newton and his wounded burden.

"It can't be done. He'll have to be chloroformed," they agreed, but just then the surgeon, Dr. Whitman, appeared.

"Newton Maxwell!" he exclaimed. "And your father and I were in college together! So you've brought in a friend who needs us, Newton." He hesitated a second. Then he motioned to an orderly to take Trusty. "It is rather a precedent to establish," he said, "but I think it can be arranged."

And it was.

Mr. Billings had a two-room cottage down near the river. It was as neat as a pin, and Emily and Newton laughed merrily when they saw Trusty's high chair, his bowl and plate marked "For a Good Dog," and a bunk by the side of the stove where he slept. It was hard for all three of them to be cheerful during the next few days, but Mr. Billing's gratitude delighted the children, and their hopes for Trusty comforted him. Mr. Billings was at his post every day, and he had never done so much business before. Everyone who had seen the little dog taking care of his master stopped to inquire how he was, and no one went on without buying an orange or an apple.

Their first Christmas opposite the hospital found Emily and Newton with only a half interest in their own gifts. They hurried through breakfast and put on their coats and caps immediately afterward ready to go down and get Mr. Billings. They ran all the way, so eager were they, calling breathlessly to each other as they went.

"Isn't it wonderful!"

"Won't he be surprised!"

But they found the blind man only half interested in the "Merry Christmas!" they shouted the moment they were inside his door. They emptied the Christmas box they had brought him and put a warm muffler, a pair of fur gloves, and a big package of fragrant coffee into his hands; but even these gifts failed to rouse him.

"I suppose we better start for the hospital soon, Mr. Billings," Newton said at last.

The blind man shook his head, feeling his way about the room and touching Trusty's bed and chair.

"I can't go," he said at last. "You've been very kind to me, and I thank you from my heart, but I can't tell you what these days have been to me without my little dog. I listen for his barking and there isn't a sound; and I can't bear to stand in the street alone, not able to reach out my hand and know that Trusty's there to lick it. We've been together ten years, Trusty and I."

Emily took Mr. Billings' hands in both of hers and entreated, although there was a catch in her voice.

"Please come, Mr. Billings. It's Christmas Day, and so many visitors will be going to the hospital and wanting to buy your fruit."

But the blind man still resisted.

"My little dog was there with me last Christmas," he said. "You don't tell me anything about him; maybe he's dead this Christmas."

"He isn't dead," Emily assured Mr. Billings.

"Please come," Newton begged. "We've got a secret about Trusty, Mr. Billings; that's why we haven't told you. Do come."

So, in the end, the children led the blind man to his place by the hospital gate.

They were exultant in their glad excitement. The children's ward had been told of the news on Christmas Eve, and it almost eclipsed the big Christmas tree, aglow with electric light bulbs and weighted down with gifts, that stood in the open space between the beds.

"You wait here, Mr. Billings," Emily and Newton said when they reached the hospital gate. "We will be out in a minute." Then they went inside the hospital to get Trusty.

Dr. Whitman himself brought Trusty to them. The dog wore a red woolen sweater, the gift of the nurses, he had a new leather collar, and a large variety of Christmas bones contributed no little to his contentment. Dr. Whitman was evidently pleased with his achievement in dog surgery and Trusty's own satisfaction was plainly seen as he took his triumphant way through the children's ward, receiving a greeting from every bed.

Outside his blind master waited. The world had never seemed so dark to him; no sun, no vision of sparkling snow and Christmas greens, no dog friend at his side—but, what was that? Mr. Billings' trained ears detected a familiar patter of feet coming down the stone pavement from the hospital. He was puzzled, though, at an unfamiliar sound. Trot, tap; trot, tap. That was the rhythm the footsteps made, coming nearer and nearer.

"Trusty?" his master called.

He put out his hand and a wet, warm tongue brushed it; then a happy wriggling, barking dog was in Mr. Billings' arms. The blind man felt for the wounded leg only to find a wooden one in its place.

"It's all right. You won't hurt him if you touch it, and he can use it just as well as he can the other three," Newton said.

"He's the very first dog in the world, I guess, to have a wooden leg." Emily added. "They had to cut off the leg that the bull dog bit, but he's got a fine, strong wooden one in its place; Dr. Whitman made Trusty as good as new!" she finished, joyously.

Tap, tap. Trusty jumped out of his master's arms and began circling around him wagging his tail as hard as he could and showing how well he could walk with his wooden leg.

"Bow, wow! I'll take you home myself tonight, dear master," Trusty seemed to say as the children left the two alone together.

"It's the jolliest Christmas we ever had, isn't it, Newton?" Emily asked.

"I should say so!" her brother said, "and all on account of living across the street from a hospital."

Countdown to Christmas   *Amy Puetz Fox*

The 12 Days of Christmas
By John Rodemeyer

The New England custom during those early years of the 1800's was to observe Christmas from December 25 to January 5, the twelve days being generally given up to receiving and returning family visits. Contemporary with this custom was the belief, inculcated in the minds of the children, that if they would visit the cow stables at midnight of Christmas Eve, they would see the cattle kneel before the mangers. A poem of the twelve days shows the gift for the first day of Christmas to be a parrot on a juniper tree instead of a "partridge on a pear tree." The verse for the twelfth day, which embodied the entire list of days and "gifts," was as follows: The twelfth day of Christmas my true love gave to me twelve guns shooting, eleven bears chasing, ten men hunting, nine fiddlers playing, eight ladies dancing, seven swans swimming, six sheets of linen, five gold rings, four coffee bowls, three French hens, two turtle doves and a parrot on a juniper tree.

Christmas Craft

Lanterns
By Susie B. Wines and Amy Puetz Fox

A string of brightly colored lanterns hung across a corner is very effective and does much toward brightening an otherwise dull or gloomy room. The material used is bright colored cardstock and old Christmas cards. The lanterns are made in various shapes. The accompanying patterns are the ones I used, but others might suggest themselves to the reader.

Enlarge the patterns below to the desired size (about 100%). Cut the cardstock or Christmas cards in the desired shape. Next bend each piece on the dotted lines, having previously drawn a sharp point over them to insure that they fold evenly. If using cardstock, you might glue part of an old Christmas card onto it to make it more attractive. Connect the edges together, using tape or glue on the flaps. Glue a string to the inside while glueing the top flaps together.

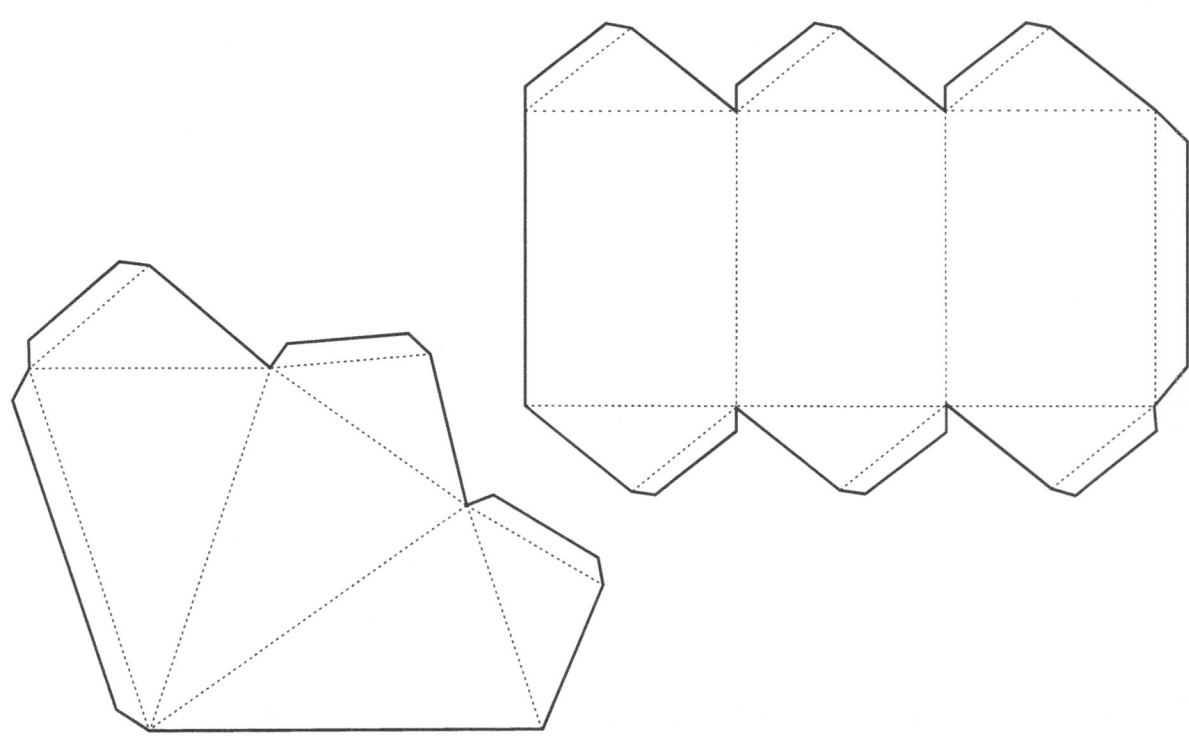

December 15

A Story of the Christ-Child

A German Legend as told by Elizabeth Harkison

Once upon a time, a long, long time ago, on the night before Christmas, a little child was wandering all alone through the streets of a great city. There were many people on the street, fathers and mothers, sisters and brothers, uncles and aunts, and even gray-haired grandfathers and grandmothers, all of whom were hurrying home with bundles of presents for each other and for their little ones. Fine carriages rolled by, express wagons rattled past, even old carts were pressed into service, and all things seemed in a hurry and glad with expectation of the coming Christmas morning.

From some of the windows bright lights were already beginning to stream until it was almost as bright as day. But the little child seemed to have no home, and wandered about listlessly from street to street. No one took any notice of him except perhaps Jack Frost, who bit his bare toes and made the ends of his fingers tingle. The north wind, too, seemed to notice the child, for it blew against him and pierced his ragged garments through and through, causing him to shiver with cold. Home after home he passed, looking with longing eyes through the windows, in upon the glad, happy children, most of whom were helping to trim the Christmas trees for the coming morrow.

"Surely," said the child to himself, "where there is so must gladness and happiness, some of it may be for me." So with timid steps he approached a large and handsome house.

Through the windows, he could see a tall and stately Christmas tree already lighted. Many presents hung upon it. Its green boughs were trimmed with gold and silver ornaments. Slowly he climbed up the broad steps and gently rapped at the door. It was opened by a large man-servant. He had a kindly face, although his voice was deep and gruff. He looked at the little child for a moment, then sadly shook his head and said, "Go down off the steps. There is no room here for such as you." He looked sorry as he spoke; possibly he remembered his own little ones at home, and was glad that they were not out in this cold and bitter night. Through the open door a bright light shone, and the warm air, filled with fragrance of the Christmas pine, rushed out from the inner room and greeted the little wanderer with a kiss. As the child turned back into the cold and darkness, he wondered why the footman had spoken thus, for surely, thought he, those little children would love to have another companion join them in their joyous Christmas festival. But the little children inside did not even know that he had knocked at the door.

The street grew colder and darker as the child passed on. He went sadly forward, saying to himself, "Is there no one in all this great city who will share the Christmas with me?" Farther and farther down the street he wandered, to where the homes were not so large and beautiful. There seemed to be little children inside of nearly all the houses. They were dancing and frolicking about. Christmas trees could be seen in nearly every window, with beautiful dolls and trumpets and picture-books and balls and tops and other dainty toys hung upon them. In one window the child noticed a little lamb made of soft white wool. Around its neck was tied a red ribbon. It had evidently been hung on the tree for one of the children. The little stranger stopped before this window and looked long and earnestly at the beautiful things inside, but most of all was he drawn toward the white lamb. At last creeping up to the windowpane, he gently tapped upon it. A little girl came to the window and looked out into the dark street where the snow had now begun to fall. She saw the child, but she only frowned and shook her head and said, "Go away and come some other time. We are too busy to take care of you now." Back into the dark, cold streets he turned again. The wind was whirling past him and seemed to say, "Hurry on, hurry on, we have no time to stop. 'Tis Christmas Eve and everybody is in a hurry tonight."

Again and again the little child rapped softly at door or windowpane. At each place he was refused admission. One mother feared he might have some ugly disease which her darlings would catch; another father said he had only enough for his own children and none to spare for beggars. Still another told him to go home where he belonged, and not to trouble other folks.

The hours passed; later grew the night, and colder grew the wind, and darker seemed the street. Farther and farther the little one wandered. There was scarcely anyone left upon the street by this time, and the few who remained did not seem to see the child, when suddenly ahead of him there appeared a bright, single ray of light. It shone through the darkness into the child's eyes. He looked up smilingly and said, "I will go where the small light beckons, perhaps they will share their Christmas with me."

Hurrying past all the other houses, he soon reached the end of the street and went straight up to the window from which the light was streaming. It was a poor, little, low house, but the child cared not for that. The light seemed still to call him in. From what do you suppose the light came? Nothing but a tallow candle which had been placed in an old cup with a broken handle, in the window, as a glad token of Christmas Eve. There was neither curtain nor shade to the small, square window and as the little child looked in he saw standing upon a neat wooden table a branch of a Christmas tree. The room was plainly furnished but it was very clean. Near the fireplace sat a lovely faced mother with a little two-year-old on her knee and an older child beside her. The two children were looking into their mother's face and listening to a story. She must have been telling them a Christmas story, I think. A few bright coals were burning in the fireplace, and all seemed light and warm within.

The little wanderer crept closer and closer to the windowpane. So sweet was the mother's face, so loving seemed the little children, that at last he took courage and tapped gently, very gently on the door. The mother stopped talking, the little children looked up. "What was that, mother?" asked the little girl at her side. "I think it was someone tapping on the door," replied the mother. "Run as quickly as you can and open it, dear, for it is a bitter cold night to keep anyone waiting in this storm." "Oh, mother, I think it was the bough of the tree tapping against the windowpane," said the little girl. "Do please go on with our story." Again the little wanderer tapped upon the door. "My child, my child," exclaimed the mother, rising, "that certainly was a rap on the door. Run quickly and open it. No one must be left out in the cold on our beautiful Christmas Eve."

The child ran to the door and threw it wide open. The mother saw the ragged stranger standing without, cold and shivering, with bare head and almost bare feet. She held out both hands and drew him into the warm, bright room. "You poor, dear child," was all she said, and putting her arms around him, she drew him close to her breast. "He is very cold, my children," she exclaimed. "We must warm him."

"And," added the little girl, "we must love him and give him some of our Christmas, too."

"Yes," said the mother, "but first let us warm him—"

The mother sat down by the fire with the little child on her lap, and her own little ones warmed his half-frozen hands in theirs. The mother smoothed his tangled curls, and, bending low over his head, kissed the child's face. She gathered the three little ones in her arms and the candle and the firelight shone over them. For a moment the room was very still. By and by the little girl said softly, to her mother, "May we not light the Christmas tree, and let him see how beautiful it looks?" "Yes," said the mother. With that she seated the child on a low stool beside the fire, and went herself to fetch the few simple ornaments which from year to year she had saved for her children's Christmas tree. They were soon so busy that they did not notice the room had filled with a strange and brilliant light. They turned and looked at the spot where the little wanderer sat. His ragged clothes had changed to garments white and beautiful; his tangled curls seemed like a halo of golden light about his head; but most glorious of all was his face, which shone with a light so dazzling that they could scarcely look upon it.

In silent wonder they gazed at the child. Their little room seemed to grow larger and larger, until it was as wide as the whole world, the roof of their low house seemed to expand and rise, until it reached to the sky.

With a sweet and gentle smile the wonderful child looked upon them for a moment, and then slowly rose and floated through the air, above the treetops, beyond the church spire, higher even than the clouds themselves, until he appeared to them to be a shining star in the sky above. At last he disappeared from sight. The astonished children turned in hushed awe to their mother, and said in a whisper, "Oh, mother, it was the Christ-Child, was it not?"

And the mother answered in a low tone, "Yes."

And it is said, dear children, that each Christmas Eve the little Christ-Child wanders through some town or village, and those who receive him and take him into their homes and hearts have given to them this marvelous vision which is denied to others.

Christmas Carols

Sing the two Christmas Carols together as a family. Discuss what the songs mean.

Away in a Manger

Martin Luther, 1483–1546   Carl Mueller

Unison

1. A-way in a manger, No crib for his bed, The little Lord Jesus Laid down his sweet head, The stars in the sky Looked down where he lay, The little Lord Jesus, A-sleep on the hay.
2. The cattle are lowing, The poor baby wakes, But little Lord Jesus, No crying he makes. I love thee, Lord Jesus, Look down from the sky, And stay by my side Until morning is nigh. A-MEN.

We Three Kings of Orient Are

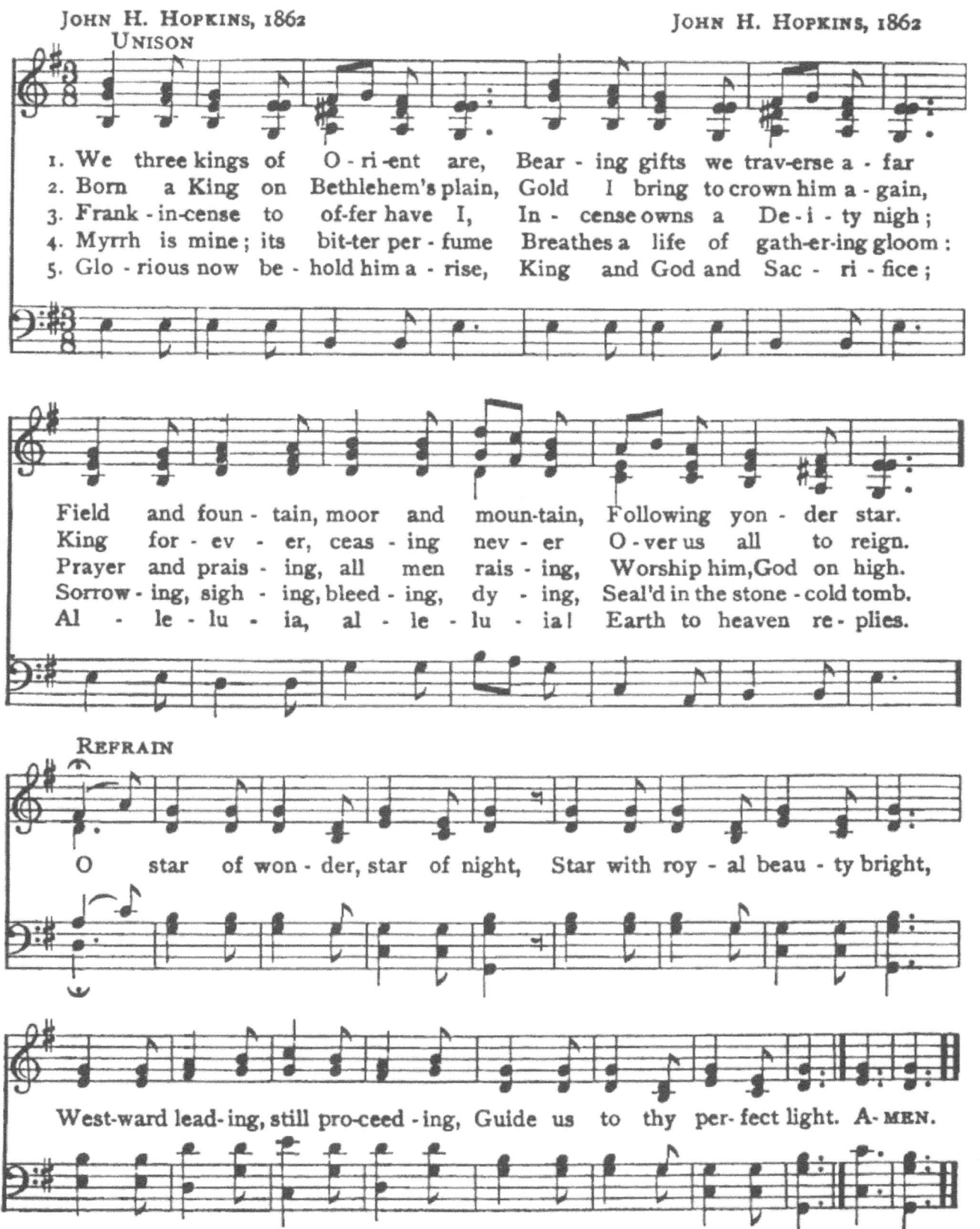

December 16

Getting a Christmas for the Little Ones

By Margaret Sidney
From Five Little Peppers and How They Grew, Chapter 16

And so October came and went. The little Peppers were very lonely after Jasper had gone; even Mrs. Pepper caught herself looking up one day when the wind blew the door open suddenly, half expecting to see the merry whole-souled boy, and the faithful dog come scampering in.

But the letters came—and that was a comfort; and it was fun to answer them. The first one spoke of Jasper's being under a private tutor, with his cousins; then they were less frequent, and they knew he was studying hard. Full of anticipations of Christmas himself, he urged the little Peppers to try for one. And the life and spirit of the letter was so catching, that Polly and Ben found their souls fired within them to try at least to get for the little ones a taste of Christmastide.

"Now, mammy," they said at last, one day in the latter part of October, when the crisp, fresh air filled their little healthy bodies with springing vitality that must bubble over and rush into something, "we don't want a Thanksgiving—truly we don't. But may we try for a Christmas—just a little one," they added, timidly, "for the children?" Ben and Polly always called the three younger ones of the flock "the children."

To their utter surprise, Mrs. Pepper looked mildly assenting, and presently she said, "Well, I don't see why you can't try; 'twon't do any harm, I'm sure."

You see Mrs. Pepper had received a letter from Jasper, which at present she didn't feel called upon to say anything about.

"Now," said Polly, drawing a long breath, as she and Ben stole away into a corner to "talk over" and lay plans, "what does it mean?"

"Never mind," said Ben; "as long as she's given us leave I don't care what it is."

"I neither," said Polly, with the delicious feeling as if the whole world were before them where to choose; "it'll be just gorgeous, Ben!"

"What's that?" asked Ben, who was not as much given to long words as Polly, who dearly loved to be fine in language as well as other things.

"Oh, it's something Jappy said one day; and I asked him, and he says it's fine, and lovely, and all that," answered Polly, delighted that she knew something she could really tell Ben.

"Then why not say fine?" commented Ben, practically, with a little upward lift of his nose.

"Oh, I'd know, I'm sure," laughed Polly. "Let's think what'll we do for Christmas—how many weeks are there, anyway, Ben?" And she began to count on her fingers.

"That's no way," said Ben, "I'm going to get the Almanac." So he went to the old clock where hanging up by its side, was a "Farmer's Almanac."

"Now, we'll know," he said, coming back to their corner. So with heads together they consulted and counted up till they found that eight weeks and three days remained in which to get ready.

"Dear me!" said Polly. "It's most a year, isn't it, Ben?"

"'Twon't be much time for us," said Ben, who thought of the many hours to be devoted to hard work that would run away with the time. "We'd better begin right away, Polly."

"Well, all right," said Polly, who could scarcely keep her fingers still, as she thought of the many things she should so love to do if she could. "But first, Ben, what let's do?"

"Would you rather hang up their stockings?" asked Ben, as if he had unlimited means at his disposal; "or have a tree?"

"Why," said Polly, with wide open eyes at the two magnificent ideas, "we haven't got anything to put in the stockings when we hang 'em, Ben."

"That's just it," said Ben. "Now, wouldn't it be better to have a tree, Polly? I can get that easy in the woods, you know."

"Well," interrupted Polly, eagerly, "we haven't got anything to hang on that, either, Ben. You know Jappy said folks hang all sorts of presents on the branches. So I don't see," she continued, impatiently, "as that's any good. We can't do anything, Ben Pepper, so there! There isn't anything to do anything with," and with a flounce Polly sat down on the old wooden stool, and folding her hands looked at Ben in a most despairing way.

"I know," said Ben, "we haven't got much."

"We haven't got anything," said Polly, still looking at him. "Why, we've got a tree," replied Ben, hopefully. "Well, what's a tree," retorted Polly, scornfully. "Anybody can go out and look at a tree outdoors."

"Well, now, I tell you, Polly," said Ben, sitting down on the floor beside her, and speaking very slowly and decisively, "we've got to do something 'cause we've begun; and we might make a tree real pretty."

"How?" asked Polly, ashamed of her ill-humor, but not in the least seeing how anything could be made of a tree. "How, Ben Pepper?"

"Well," said Ben, pleasantly, "we'd set it up in the corner—"

"Oh, no, not in the corner," cried Polly, whose spirits began to rise a little as she saw Ben so hopeful. "Put it in the middle of the room, do!"

"I don't care where you put it," said Ben, smiling, happy that Polly's usual cheerful energy had returned, "but I thought—'twill be a little one, you know, and I thought 'twould look better in the corner."

"What else?" asked Polly, eager to see how Ben would dress the tree.

"Well," said Ben, "you know the Henderson boys gave me a lot of corn last week."

"I don't see as that helps much," said Polly, still incredulous. "Do you mean hang the cobs on the branches, Ben? That would be just dreadful!"

"I should think likely," laughed Ben. "No, indeed, Polly Pepper! But if we should pop a lot, oh! A bushel—and then we should string 'em, we could wind it all in and out among the branches, and—."

"Why, wouldn't that be pretty?" cried Polly, "real pretty—and we can do that, I'm sure."

"Yes," continued Ben; "and then, don't you know, there's some little candle ends in that box in the Provision Room, maybe mammy'd give us them."

"I don't believe but she would," cried Polly; "twould be just like Jappy's if she would! Let's ask her now—this very same minute!"

And they scampered hurriedly to Mrs. Pepper, who to their extreme astonishment, after all, said "yes," and smiled encouragingly on the plan.

"Isn't mammy good?" said Polly, with loving gratitude, as they seated themselves again.

"Now we're all right," exclaimed Ben, "and I tell you we can make the tree look perfectly splendid, Polly Pepper!"

"And I'll tell you another thing, Ben," Polly said, "Oh! Something elegant! You must get ever so many hickory nuts; and you know those bits of bright paper I've got in the bureau drawer? Well, we can paste them on to the nuts and hang 'em on for the balls Jappy tells of."

"Polly," cried Ben, "it'll be such a tree as never was, won't it?"

"Yes; but dear me," cried Polly, springing up, "the children are coming! Wasn't it good, grandma wanted 'em to come over this afternoon, so's we could talk! Now hush!" as the door opened to admit the noisy little troop.

"If you think of any new plan," whispered Ben, behind his hand, while Mrs. Pepper engaged their attention, "you'll have to come out into the woodshed to talk after this."

"I know it," whispered Polly back again; "Oh! we've got just heaps of things to think of, Bensie!"

Such a contriving and racking of brains as Polly and Ben set up after this! They would bob over at each other, and smile with significant gesture as a new idea would strike one of them, in the most mysterious way that, if observed, would drive the others almost wild. And then, frightened lest in some hilarious moment the secret should pop out, the two conspirators would betake themselves to the woodshed as before agreed on. But Joel, finding this out, followed them one day—or, as Polly said, tagged—so that was no good.

"Let's go behind the woodpile," she said to Ben, in desperation; "he can't hear there, if we whisper real soft."

"Yes, he will," said Ben, who knew Joel's hearing faculties much better. "We'll have to wait till they're a-bed."

So after that, when nightfall first began to make its appearance, Polly would hint mildly about bedtime.

"You hustle us so!" said Joel, after he had been sent off to bed for two or three nights unusually early.

"Oh, Joey, it's good for you to get to bed," said Polly, coaxingly; "it'll make you grow, you know, real fast."

"Well, I don't grow a-bed," grumbled Joel, who thought something was in the wind. "You and Ben are going to talk, I know, and wink your eyes, as soon as we're gone."

"Well, go along, Joe, that's a good boy," said Polly, laughing, "and you'll know someday."

"What'll you give me?" asked Joel, seeing a bargain, his foot on the lowest stair leading to the loft, "say, Polly?"

"Oh, I haven't got much to give," she said, cheerily; "but I'll tell you what, Joey—I'll tell you a story every day that you go to bed."

"Will you?" cried Joe, hopping back into the room. "Begin now, Polly, begin now!"

"Why, you haven't been to bed yet," said Polly, "so I can't till tomorrow."

"Yes, I have—you've made us go for three—no, I guess fourteen nights," said Joel, indignantly.

"Well, you were made to go," laughed Polly. "I said if you'd go good, you know; so run along, Joe, and I'll tell you a nice one tomorrow."

"It's got to be long," shouted Joel, when he saw he could get no more, making good time up to the loft.

To say that Polly, in the following days, was Master Joel's slave, was stating the case lightly. However, she thought by her story-telling she got off easily, as each evening saw the boys drag their unwilling feet to-bedward, and leave Ben and herself in peace to plan and work undisturbed. There they would sit by the little old table, around the one tallow candle, while Mrs. Pepper sewed away busily, looking up to smile or to give some bits of advice; keeping her own secret meanwhile, which made her blood leap fast, as the happy thoughts nestled in her heart of her little ones and their coming glee. And Polly made the loveliest of paper dolls for Phronsie out of the rest of the bits of bright paper; and Ben made windmills and whistles for the boys; and a funny little carved basket with a handle, for Phronsie, out of a hickory nut shell; and a new pink calico dress for Seraphina peered out from the top drawer of the old bureau in the bedroom, whenever anyone opened it—for Mrs. Pepper kindly let the children lock up their treasures there as fast as completed.

"I'll make Seraphina a bonnet," said Mrs. Pepper, "for there's that old bonnet-string in the bag, you know, Polly, that'll make it beautiful."

"Oh, do, mother," cried Polly, "she's been wanting a new one awfully."

"And I'm going to knit some mittens for Joel and David," continued Mrs. Pepper; "cause I can get the yarn cheap now. I saw some down at the store yesterday I could have at half price."

"I don't believe anybody'll have as good a Christmas as we shall," cried Polly, pasting on a bit of trimming to the prettiest doll's dress; "no, not even Jappy."

An odd little smile played around Mrs. Pepper's mouth, but she said not a word, and so the fun and the work went on.

The tree was to be set up in the Provision Room; that was finally decided, as Mrs. Pepper showed the children how utterly useless it would be to try having it in the kitchen.

"I'll find the key, children," she said, "I think I know where 'tis, and then we can keep them out."

"Well, but it looks so," said Polly, demurring at the prospect.

"Oh, no, Polly," said her mother; "at any rate it's clean."

"Polly," said Ben, "we can put evergreen around, you know,

"So we can," said Polly, brightly; "Oh, Ben, you do think of the best things; we couldn't have had them in the kitchen."

"And don't let's hang the presents on the tree," continued Ben; "let's have the children hang up their stockings; they want to, awfully—

for I heard David tell Joel this morning before we got up—they thought I was asleep, but I wasn't—that he did so wish they could, but, says he, 'Don't tell mammy, 'cause that'll make her feel bad.'"

"The little dears!" said Mrs. Pepper, impulsively; "they shall have their stockings, too."

"And we'll make the tree pretty enough," said Polly, enthusiastically; "we shan't want the presents to hang on; we've got so many things. And then we'll have hickory nuts to eat; and perhaps mammy'll let us make some molasses candy the day before," she said, with a sly look at her mother.

"You may," said Mrs. Pepper, smiling.

"Oh, goody!" they both cried, hugging each other ecstatically.

"And we'll have a frolic in the Provision Room afterwards," finished Polly; "Oh! Ooh!"

And so the weeks flew by—one, two, three, four, five, six, seven, eight! Till only the three days remained, and to think the fun that Polly and Ben had had already!

"It's better'n a Christmas," they told their mother, "to get ready for it!"

"It's too bad you can't hang up your stockings," said Mrs. Pepper, looking keenly at their flushed faces and bright eyes; "you've never hung 'em up."

"That isn't any matter, mamsie," they both said, cheerily; "it's a great deal better to have the children have a nice time—oh, won't it be elegant! P'r'aps we'll have ours next year!"

For two days before, the house was turned upside down for Joel to find the biggest stocking he could; but on Polly telling him it must be his own, he stopped his search, and bringing down his well-worn one, hung it by the corner of the chimney to be ready.

"You put yours up the other side, Dave," he advised.

"There isn't any nail," cried David, investigating.

"I'll drive one," said Joel, so he ran out to the tool house, as one corner of the woodshed was called, and brought in the hammer and one or two nails.

"Phronsie's a-goin' in the middle," he said, with a nail in his mouth.

"Yes, I'm a-goin' to hang up my stockin'," cried the child, hopping from one toe to the other.

"Run get it, Phronsie," said Joel, "and I'll hang it up for you.

"Why, it's two days before Christmas yet," said Polly, laughing; "how they'll look hanging there so long."

"I don't care," said Joel, giving a last thump to the nail; "we're a-goin' to be ready. Oh, dear! I wish 'twas tonight!"

"Can't Seraphina hang up her stocking?" asked Phronsie, coming up to Polly's side; "and Baby, too?"

"Oh, let her have part of yours," said Polly, "that'll be best—Seraphina and Baby, and you have one stocking together."

"Oh, yes," cried Phronsie, easily pleased; "that'll be best." So for the next two days, they were almost distracted; the youngest ones asking countless questions about Santa Claus, and how he possibly could get down the chimney. Joel running his head up as far as he dared, to see if it was big enough.

"I guess he can," he said, coming back in a sooty state, looking very much excited and delighted.

"Will he be black like Joey?" asked Phronsie, pointing to his grimy face.

"No," said Polly; "he don't ever get black."

"Why?" they all asked; and then, over and over, they wanted the delightful mystery explained.

"We never'll get through this day," said Polly in despair, as the last one arrived. "I wish 'twas tonight, for we're all ready."

"Santy's coming! Santy's coming!" sang Phronsie, as the bright afternoon sunlight went down over the fresh, crisp snow, "for it's night now."

"Yes, Santa is coming!" sang Polly; and "Santa Claus is coming," rang back and forth through the old kitchen, till it seemed as if the three little old stockings would hop down and join in the dance going on so merrily.

"I'm glad mine is red," said Phronsie, at last, stopping in the wild jig, and going up to see if it was all safe, "cause then Santy'll know it's mine, won't he, Polly?"

"Yes, dear," cried Polly, catching her up. "Oh, Phronsie! you are going to have a Christmas!"

"Well, I wish," said Joel, "I had my name on mine! I know Dave'll get some of my things."

"Oh, no, Joe," said Mrs. Pepper, "Santa Claus is smart; he'll know yours is in the left-hand corner."

"Will he?" asked Joel, still a little fearful.

"Oh, yes, indeed," said Mrs. Pepper, confidently. "I never knew him to make a mistake."

"Now," said Ben, when they had all made a pretence of eating supper, for there was such an excitement prevailing that no one sat still long enough to eat much, "you must every one fly off to bed as quick as ever can be."

"Will Santa Claus come faster then?" asked Joel.

"Yes," said Ben, "just twice as fast."

"I'm going, then," said Joel; "but I ain't going to sleep, 'cause I mean to hear him come over the roof; then I'm going to get up, for I do so want a squint at the reindeer!"

"I am, too," cried Davie, excitedly. "Oh, do come, Joe!" and he began to mount the stairs.

"Good night," said Phronsie, going up to the center of the chimney-piece, where the little red stocking dangled limpsily, "lift me up, Polly, do."

"What you want to do?" asked Polly, running and giving her a jump. "What you goin' to do, Phronsie?"

"I want to kiss it good night," said the child, with eyes big with anticipation and happiness, hugging the well worn toe of the little old stocking affectionately. "I wish I had something to give Santa, Polly, I do!" she cried, as she held her fast in her arms.

"Never mind, Pet," said Polly, nearly smothering her with kisses; "if you're a good girl, Phronsie, that pleases Santa the most of anything."

"Does it?" cried Phronsie, delighted beyond measure, as Polly carried her into the bedroom, "then I'll be good always, I will!"

To be continued . . .

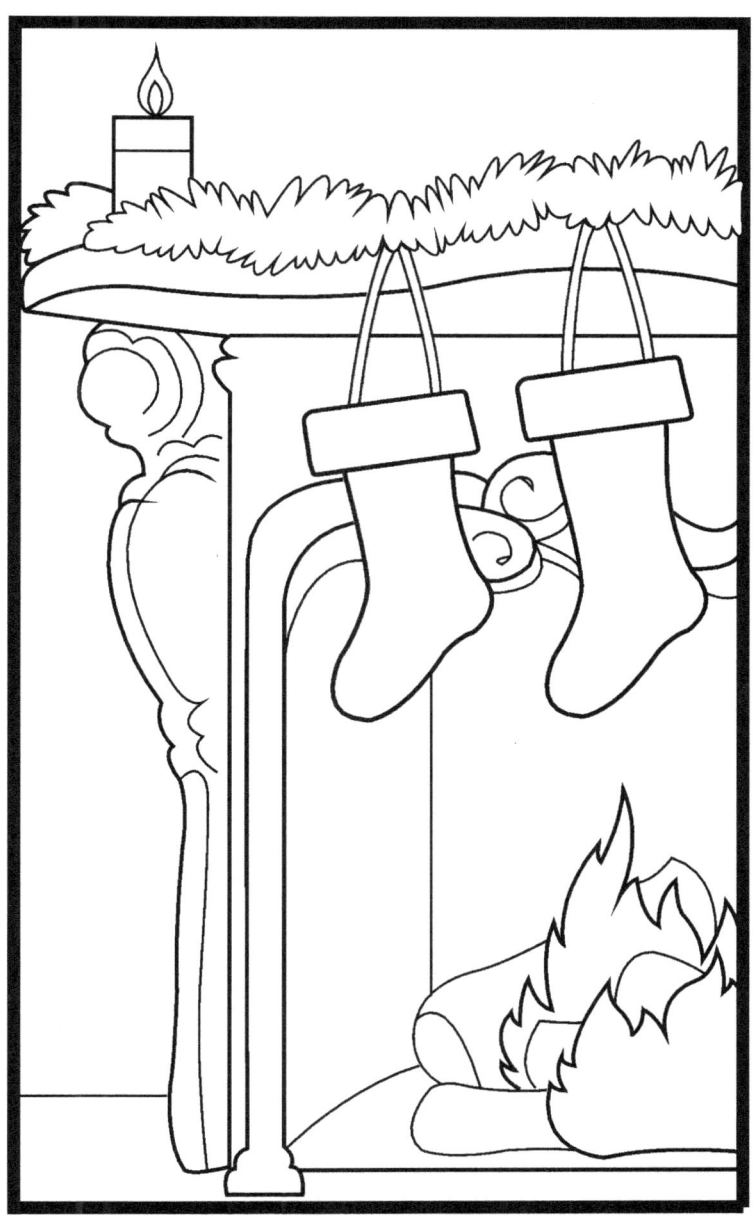

Christmas Games

Buz by Laura Valentine

This is a very old game. The players sit in a circle, and count, beginning at one and going on to a hundred, which must, if possible, be reached. But the number "seven" must not be mentioned, Buz being substituted for it. For instance, the players say alternately, "one," "two," "three," "four," "five," "six;" the seventh exclaims, "Buz;" the others go on, "eight," "nine," "ten," "eleven," "twelve," "thirteen," "Buz" (because twice seven make fourteen), "fifteen," "sixteen," "Buz" (for seventeen), "eighteen," "nineteen," "twenty," "Buz" (because three times seven are twenty-one).

Thus Buz is said whenever a seven is named, or a number out of the line of seven times in the multiplication table, as fourteen, twenty-one, twenty-eight, thirty-five, forty-two, forty-nine, fifty-six, sixty-three, seventy, etc. When the players reach seventy-one, they must say, "Buz one," "Buz two," etc.

Rules of the game:

1st Rule—Buz is to be said for every seven, or number in "seven times."

2nd Rule—Any one breaking 1st Rule is out of the game.

3rd Rule—Directly a "seven," or seven times number has been named, the counting must begin again; the one sitting on the left hand of the expelled member beginning again with "one."

4th Rule—If any player forgets his or her number while the counting is going on, or miscounts after a Buz, he or she is out of the game. This game must be played quickly, and it will be found that Buz will so often be forgotten in its right place that the number of players, will continually diminish, till it ends sometimes only in a pair. And, as after every blunder the count begins again at "one," it is a matter of some difficulty to reach a hundred. We recommend this game as a very merry and pleasant one.

For elder players this game may be made much more amusing by saying Fiz, instead of five and its multiples. Example: One, two three, four, Fiz, six, Buz, etc. Thus fifty-seven would be Fiz-Buz.

Musical Chairs by Laura Valentine and Amy Puetz Fox

Place a number of chairs one less than the number of players in a circle. One person plays either a musical CD or musical instrument with his or her back to the group. The group walks around the chairs while the music is playing. The person playing the music stops unexpectedly and each person tries to sit down. One person is left standing and is out of the game. Another chair is removed from the circle and the music begins again. Continue playing the game in this way until only two people remain with one chair. Whoever is the last person to sit down wins and gets to be in charge of the music for the next round.

December 17

Christmas Bells!
By Margaret Sidney
From Five Little Peppers and How They Grew, Chapter 17

In the middle of the night Polly woke up with a start.

"What in the world!" said she, and she bobbed up her head and looked over at her mother, who was still peacefully sleeping, and was just going to lie down again, when a second noise out in the kitchen made her pause and lean on her elbow to listen. At this moment she thought she heard a faint whisper, and springing out of bed she ran to Phronsie's crib—it was empty! As quick as a flash she sped out into the kitchen. There, in front of the chimney, were two figures. One was Joel, and the other, unmistakably, was Phronsie!

"What are you doing?" gasped Polly, holding on to a chair.

The two little nightgowns turned around at this.

"Why, I thought it was morning," said Joel, "and I wanted my stocking. Oh!" as he felt the toe, which was generously stuffed "give it to me, Polly Pepper, and I'll run right back to bed again!"

"Dear me!" said Polly; "and you, too, Phronsie! Why, it's the middle of the night! Did I ever!" and she had to pinch her mouth together tight to keep from bursting out into a loud laugh. "Oh, dear, I shall laugh! Don't look so scared, Phronsie, there won't anything hurt you." For Phronsie who, on hearing Joel fumbling around the precious stockings, had been quite willing to hop out of bed and join him, had now, on Polly's saying the dire words "in the middle of the night," scuttled over to her protecting side like a frightened rabbit.

"It never'll be morning," said Joel taking up first one cold toe and then the other; "you might let us have 'em now, Polly."

"No," said Polly sobering down; "you can't have yours till Davie wakes up, too. Scamper off to bed, Joey, dear, and forget all about 'em—and it'll be morning before you know it."

"Oh, I'd rather go to bed," said Phronsie, trying to tuck up her feet in the little flannel night-gown, which was rather short, "but I don't know the way back, Polly. Take me, Polly, do," and she put up her arms to be carried.

"Oh, I ain't a-goin' back alone, either," whimpered Joel, coming up to Polly, too.

"Why, you came down alone, didn't you?" whispered Polly, with a little laugh.

"Yes, but I thought 'twas morning," said Joel, his teeth chattering with something beside the cold.

"Well, you must think of the morning that's coming," said Polly, cheerily. "I'll tell you—you wait till I put Phronsie into the crib, and then I'll come back and go halfway up the stairs with you."

"I won't never come down till it's mornin' again," said Joel, bouncing along the stairs, when Polly was ready to go with him, at a great rate.

"Better not," laughed Polly, softly. "Be careful and not wake Davie nor Ben."

"I'm in," announced Joel, in a loud whisper; and Polly could hear him snuggle down among the warm bedclothes. "Call us when 'tis mornin', Polly."

"Yes," said Polly, "I will; go to sleep."

Phronsie had forgotten stockings and everything else on Polly's return, and was fast asleep in the old crib. The result of it was that the children slept over, when morning did really come; and Polly had to keep her promise, and go to the foot of the stairs and call—"MERRY CHRISTMAS! Oh, Ben! And Joel! And Davie!"

"Oh!—Oh!—Oo-h!" and then the sounds that answered her, as with smothered whoops of expectation they one and all flew into their clothes!

Quick as a flash Joel and Davie were down and dancing around the chimney.

"Mammy! Mammy!" screamed Phronsie, hugging her stocking, which Ben lifted her up to unhook from the big nail, "Santy did come, he did!" and then she spun around in the middle of the floor, not stopping to look in it.

"Well, open it, Phronsie," called Davie, deep in the exploring of his own; "Oh! Isn't that a splendid windmill, Joe?"

"Yes," said that individual, who, having found a big piece of molasses candy, was so engaged in enjoying a huge bite that, regardless alike of his other gifts or of the smearing his face was getting, he gave himself wholly up to its delights.

"Oh, Joey," cried Polly, laughingly, "molasses candy for breakfast!"

"That's prime!" cried Joel, swallowing the last morsel. "Now I'm going to see what's this—oh, Dave, see here! See here!" he cried in intense excitement, pulling out a nice little parcel which, unrolled, proved to be a bright pair of stout mittens. "See if you've got some—look quick!"

"Yes, I have," said David, picking up a parcel about as big. "No, that's molasses candy."

"Just the same as I had," said Joel; "do look for the mittens. P'r'aps Santa Claus thought you had some—oh, dear!"

"Here they are!" screamed Davie. "I have got some, Joe, just exactly like yours! See, Joe!"

"Goody!" said Joel, immensely relieved; for now he could quite enjoy his to see a pair on Davie's hands, also. "Look at Phron," he cried, "she hasn't got only half of her things out!"

To tell the truth, Phronsie was so bewildered by her riches that she sat on the floor with the little red stocking in her lap, laughing and cooing to herself amid the few things she had drawn out. When she came to Seraphina's bonnet she was quite overcome. She turned it over and over, and smoothed out the little white feather that had once adorned one of Grandma Bascom's chickens, until the two boys with their stockings, and the others sitting around in a group on the floor watching them, laughed in glee to see her enjoyment.

"Oh, dear," said Joel, at last, shaking his stocking; "I've got all there is. I wish there were forty Christmases coming!"

"I haven't!" screamed Davie; "there's something in the toe."

"It's an apple, I guess," said Joel; "turn it up, Dave."

"'Tisn't an apple," exclaimed Davie, "'tisn't round—it's long and thin; here 'tis." And he pulled out a splendid long whistle on which he blew a blast long and terrible, and Joel immediately following, all quiet was broken up, and the wildest hilarity reigned.

"I don't know as you'll want any breakfast," at last said Mrs. Pepper, when she had got Phronsie a little sobered down.

"I do, I do!" cried Joel.

"Dear me! After your candy?" said Polly.

"That's all gone," said Joel, tooting around the table on his whistle. "What are we going to have for breakfast?"

"Same as ever," said his mother; "it can't be Christmas all the time."

"I wish 'twas," said little Davie; "forever and ever!"

"Forever an' ever," echoed little Phronsie, flying up, her cheeks like two pinks, and Seraphina in her arms with her bonnet on upside down.

"Dear, dear," said Polly, pinching Ben to keep still as they tumbled down the little rickety steps to the Provision Room, after breakfast. The children, content in their treasures, were holding high carnival in the kitchen. "Suppose they should find it out now—I declare I should feel most awfully. Isn't it elegant?" she asked, in a subdued whisper, going all around and around the tree, magnificent in its dress of bright red and yellow balls, white festoons, and little candle-ends all ready for lighting. "Oh, Ben, did you lock the door?"

"Yes," he said. "That's a mouse," he added, as a little rustling noise made Polly stop where she stood back of the tree and prick up her ears in great distress of mind. "'Tis elegant," he said, turning around in admiration, and taking in the tree which, as Polly said, was quite "gorgeous," and the evergreen branches twisted up on the beams and rafters, and all the other festive arrangements. "Even Jappy's isn't better, I don't believe!"

"I wish Jappy was here," said Polly with a small sigh.

"Well, he isn't," said Ben; "come, we must go back into the kitchen, or all the children will be out here. Look your last, Polly; 'twon't do to come again till it's time to light up."

"Mammy says she'd rather do the lighting up," said Polly. "Had she?" said Ben, in surprise;

"Oh, I suppose she's afraid we'll set somethin' a-fire. Well, then, we shan't come in till we have it."

"I can't bear to go," said Polly, turning reluctantly away; "it's most beautiful—oh, Ben," and she faced him for the five-hundredth time with the question, "is your Santa Claus dress all safe?"

"Yes," said Ben, "I'll warrant they won't find that in one hurry! Such a time as we've had to make it!"

"I know it," laughed Polly; "don't that cotton wool look just like bits of fur, Ben?"

"Yes," said Ben, "and when the flour's shaken over me it'll be Santa himself."

"We've got to put back the hair into mamsie's cushion the first thing tomorrow," whispered Polly anxiously, "and we mustn't forget it, Bensie."

"I want to keep the wig awfully," said Ben. "You did make that just magnificent, Polly!"

"If you could see yourself," giggled Polly; "did you put it in the straw bed? And are you sure you pulled the ticking over it smooth?"

"Yes, sir," replied Ben, "sure's my name's Ben Pepper! If you'll only keep them from seeing me when I'm in it till we're ready—that's all I ask."

"Well," said Polly a little relieved, "but I hope Joe won't look."

"Come on! They're a-comin'!" whispered Ben; "Quick!"

"Polly!" rang a voice dangerously near; so near that Polly, speeding over the stairs to intercept it, nearly fell on her nose.

"Where you been?" asked one.

"Let's have a concert," put in Ben; Polly was so out of breath that she couldn't speak. "Come, now, each take a whistle, and we'll march round and round and see which can make the biggest noise."

In the rattle and laughter which this procession made all mystery was forgotten, and the two conspirators began to breathe freer.

Five o'clock! The small ones of the Pepper flock, being pretty well tired out with noise and excitement, all gathered around Polly and Ben, and clamored for a story.

"Do, Polly, do," begged Joel. "It's Christmas, and 'twon't come again for a year."

"I can't," said Polly, in such a twitter that she could hardly stand still, and for the first time in her life refusing, "I can't think of a thing."

"I will then," said Ben; "we must do something," he whispered to Polly.

"Tell it good," said Joel, settling himself.

So for an hour the small tyrants kept their entertainers well employed.

"Isn't it growing awful dark?" said Davie, rousing himself at last, as Ben paused to take breath.

Polly pinched Ben.

"Mammy's a-goin' to let us know," he whispered in reply. "We must keep on a little longer."

"Don't stop," said Joel, lifting his head where he sat on the floor. "What you whisperin' for, Polly?"

"I'm not," said Polly, glad to think she hadn't spoken.

"Well, do go on, Ben," said Joel, lying down again.

"Polly'll have to finish it," said Ben; "I've got to go upstairs now."

So Polly launched out into such an extravagant story that they all, perforce, had to listen.

All this time Mrs. Pepper had been pretty busy in her way. And now she came into the kitchen and set down her candle on the table. "Children," she said. Everybody turned and looked at her—her tone was so strange; and when they saw her dark eyes shining with such a new light, little Davie skipped right out into the middle of the room. "What's the matter, mammy?"

"You may all come into the Provision Room," said she.

"What for?" shouted Joel, in amazement; while the others jumped to their feet, and stood staring.

Polly flew around like a general, arranging her forces. "Let's march there," said she; "Phronsie, you take hold of Davie's hand, and go first."

"I'm goin' first," announced Joel, squeezing up past Polly. "No, you mustn't, Joe," said Polly decidedly; "Phronsie and David are the youngest."

"They're always the youngest," said Joel, falling back with Polly to the rear.

"Forward! MARCH!" sang Polly. "Follow mamsie!"

Down the stairs they went with military step, and into the Provision Room. And then, with one wild look, the little battalion broke ranks, and tumbling one over the other in decidedly unmilitary style, presented a very queer appearance!

And Captain Polly was the queerest of all; for she just gave one gaze at the tree, and then sat right down on the floor, and said, "Oh! OH!"

Mrs. Pepper was flying around delightedly, and saying, "Please to come right in," and "How do you do?"

And before anybody knew it, there were the laughing faces of Mrs. Henderson and the Parson himself, Doctor Fisher and old Grandma Bascom; while the two Henderson boys, unwilling to be defrauded of any of the fun, were squeezing themselves in between everybody else, and coming up to Polly every third minute, and saying, "There—aren't you surprised?"

"It's Fairyland!" cried little Davie, out of his wits with joy; "Oh! Aren't we in Fairyland, Ma?"

The whole room was in one buzz of chatter and fun; and everybody beamed on everybody else; and nobody knew what they said, till Mrs. Pepper called, "Hush! Santa Claus is coming!"

A rattle at the little old window made everybody look there, just as a great snow-white head popped up over the sill.

"Oh!" screamed Joel, "'Tis Santy!"

"He's a-comin' in!" cried Davie in chorus, which sent Phronsie flying to Polly. In jumped a little old man, quite spry for his years; with a jolly, red face and a pack on his back, and flew into their midst, prepared to do his duty; but what should he do, instead of making his speech, "This jolly Old Saint—" but first fly up to Mrs. Pepper, and say—"Oh, mammy how did you do it?"

"It's Ben!" screamed Phronsie; but the little Old Saint didn't hear, for he and Polly took hold of hands, and pranced around that tree while everybody laughed till they cried to see them go!

And then it all came out!

"Order!" said Parson Henderson in his deepest tones; and then he put into Santa Claus' hands a letter, which he requested him to read. And the jolly Old Saint, although he was very old, didn't need any spectacles, but piped out in Ben's loudest tones:

"Dear Friends—A Merry Christmas to you all! And that you'll have a good time, and enjoy it all as much as I've enjoyed my good times at your house, is the wish of your friend,

Jasper Elyot King"

"Hurrah for Jappy!" cried Santa Claus, pulling his beard; and "Hurrah for Jasper!" went all around the room; and this ended in three good cheers—Phronsie coming in too late with her little crow—which was just as well, however!

"Do your duty now, Santa Claus!" commanded Dr. Fisher as master of ceremonies; and everything was as still as a mouse!

And the first thing she knew, a lovely brass cage, with a dear little bird with two astonished black eyes dropped down into Polly's hands. The card on it said: "For Miss Polly Pepper, to give her music every day in the year."

"Mammy," said Polly; and then she did the queerest thing of the whole! She just burst into tears! "I never thought I should have a bird for my very own!"

"Hulloa!" said Santa Claus, "I've got something myself!"

"Santa Claus' clothes are too old," laughed Dr. Fisher, holding up a stout, warm suit that a boy about as big as Ben would delight in.

And then that wonderful tree just rained down all manner of lovely fruit. Gifts came flying thick and fast, till the air seemed full, and each one was greeted with a shout of glee, as it was put into the hands of its owner. A shawl flew down on Mrs. Pepper's shoulders; and a work-basket tumbled on Polly's head; and tops and balls and fishing poles, sent Joel and David into a corner with howls of delight!

But the climax was reached when a large wax doll in a very pretty pink silk dress, was put into Phronsie's hands, and Dr. Fisher, stooping down, read in loud tones: "For Phronsie, from one who enjoyed her gingerbread boy."

After that, nobody had anything to say! Books jumped down unnoticed, and pretty boxes of candy. Only Polly peeped into one of her books, and saw in Jappy's plain hand—"I hope we'll both read this next summer." And turning over to the title-page, she saw "A Complete Manual of Cookery."

"The best is to come," said Mrs. Henderson in her gentle way. When there was a lull in the gale, she took Polly's hand, and led her to a little stand of flowers in the corner concealed by a sheet— pinks and geraniums, heliotropes and roses, blooming away, and nodding their pretty heads at the happy sight—Polly had her flowers.

"Why didn't we know?" cried the children at last, when everybody was tying on their hoods, and getting their hats to leave the festive scene, "how could you keep it secret, mammy?"

"They all went to Mrs. Henderson's," said Mrs. Pepper; "Jasper wrote me, and asked where to send 'em, and Mrs. Henderson was so kind as to say that they might come there. And we brought 'em over last evening, when you were all abed. I couldn't have done it," she said, bowing to the Parson and his wife, "if 'twasn't for their kindness—never, in all this world!"

"And I'm sure," said the minister, looking around on the bright group, "if we can help along a bit of happiness like this, it is a blessed thing!"

And here Joel had the last word. "You said 'twan't goin' to be Christmas always, mammy. I say," looking around on the overflow of treasures and the happy faces—"it'll be just forever!"

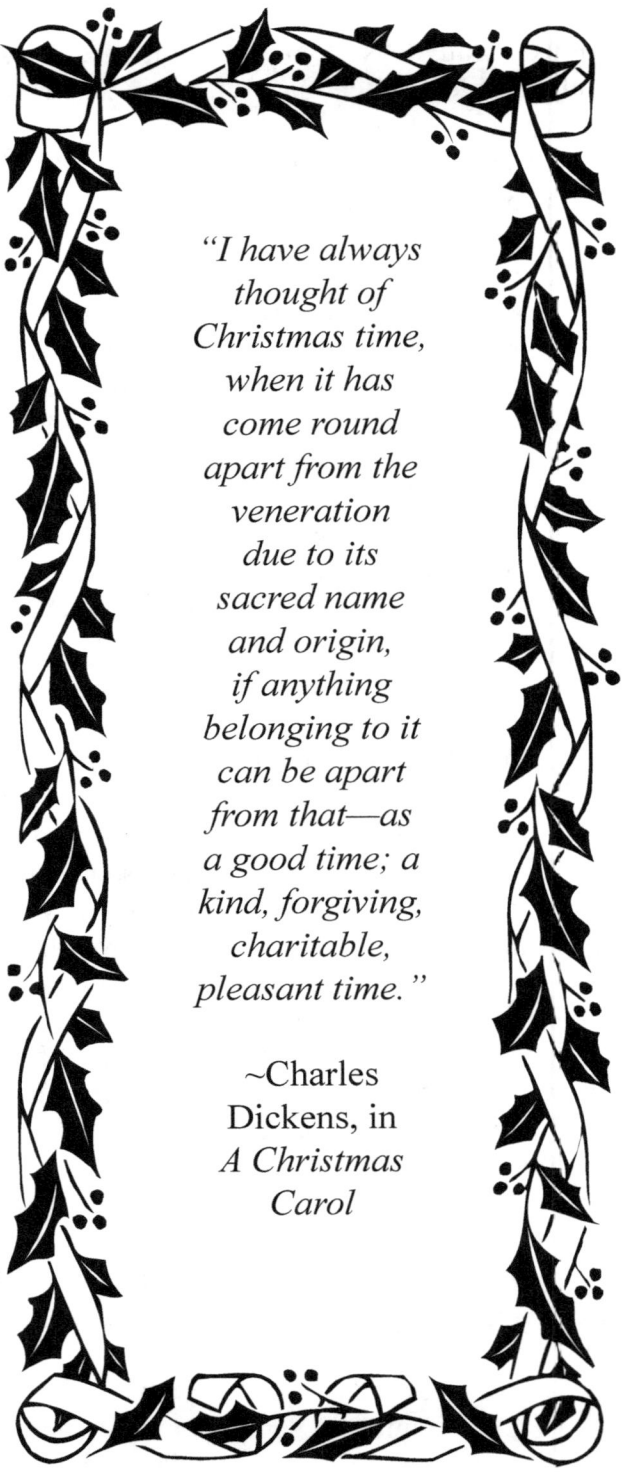

"I have always thought of Christmas time, when it has come round apart from the veneration due to its sacred name and origin, if anything belonging to it can be apart from that—as a good time; a kind, forgiving, charitable, pleasant time."

~Charles Dickens, in *A Christmas Carol*

Christmas Carols

Sing the two Christmas Carols together as a family. Discuss what the songs mean.

Deck the Hall with Boughs of Holly

Welsh Air.

1. Deck the hall with boughs of hol-ly,
   'Tis the sea-son to be jol-ly,
   Fa la la la la la la la la,
   Don we now our gay ap-par-el,
   Troll the ancient Christmas car-ol,
   Fa la la la la la la la la.

2. See the blaz-ing yule be-fore us,
   Strike the harp and join the chorus,
   Fa la la la la la la la la,
   Follow me in mer-ry measure,
   While I tell of Christmas treasure,
   Fa la la la la la la la la.

3. Fast a-way the old year pass-es,
   Hail the new, ye lads and lasses!
   Fa la la la la la la la la,
   Sing we joy-ous all to-geth-er,
   Heedless of the wind and weather.
   Fa la la la la la la la la.

Silent Night

MICHAEL HAYDN.

1. Silent night! Holy night! All is calm, all is bright
2. Silent night! Holy night! Shepherds quake at the sight!
3. Silent night! Holy night! Son of god, love's pure light

Round yon virgin mother and Child! Holy Infant, so tender and mild,
Glories stream from Heaven afar Heavenly hosts sing Alleluia.
Radiant beams from Thy holy face, With the dawn of redeeming grace,

Sleep in heavenly peace, Sleep in heavenly peace.
Christ, the Saviour, is born! Christ, the Saviour, is born!
Jesus, Lord, at thy birth, Jesus, Lord, at thy birth.

December 18

The Legend of Babouscka
Adapted from a Russian Tale

It was the night the dear Christ-Child came to Bethlehem. In a country far away from Him, an old, old woman named Babouscka sat in her snug little house by her warm fire. The wind was drifting the snow outside and howling down the chimney, but it only made Babouscka's fire burn more brightly.

"How glad I am that I may stay indoors," said Babouscka, holding her hands out to the bright blaze.

But suddenly she heard a loud rap at her door. She opened it and her candle shone on three old men standing outside in the snow. Their beards were as white as the snow, and so long that they reached the ground. Their eyes shone kindly in the light of Babouscka's candle, and their arms were full of precious things—boxes of jewels, and sweet-smelling oils, and ointments.

"We have traveled far, Babouscka," they said, "and we stop to tell you of the Baby Prince born this night in Bethlehem. He comes to rule the world and teach all men to be loving and true. We carry Him gifts. Come with us, Babouscka."

But Babouscka looked at the drifting snow, and then inside at her cozy room and the crackling fire. "It is too late for me to go with you, good sirs," she said, "the weather is too cold." She went inside again and shut the door, and the old men journeyed on to Bethlehem without her. But as Babouscka sat by her fire, rocking, she began to think about the Little Christ-Child, for she loved all babies.

"Tomorrow I will go to find Him," she said; "tomorrow, when it is light, and I will carry Him some toys."

So when it was morning Babouscka put on her long cloak and took her staff, and filled her basket with the pretty things a baby would like—gold balls, and wooden toys, and strings of silver cobwebs and she set out to find the Christ-Child.

But, oh, Babouscka had forgotten to ask the three old men the road to Bethlehem, and they traveled so far through the night that she could not overtake them. Up and down the road she hurried, through woods and fields and towns, saying to whomsoever she met: "I go to find the Christ-Child. Where does He lie? I bring some pretty toys for His sake."

But no one could tell her the way to go, and they all said: "Farther on, Babouscka, farther on." So she traveled on and on and on for years and years—but she never found the little Christ-Child.

They say that old Babouscka is traveling still, looking for Him. When it comes Christmas Eve, and the children are lying fast asleep, Babouscka comes softly through the snowy fields and towns, wrapped in her long cloak and carrying her basket on her arm. With her staff she raps gently at the doors and goes inside and holds her candle close to the little children's faces.

"Is He here?" she asks. "Is the little Christ-Child here?" And then she turns sorrowfully away again, crying: "Farther on, farther on!" But before she leaves she takes a toy from her basket and lays it beside the pillow for a Christmas gift. "For His sake," she says softly, and then hurries on through the years and forever in search of the little Christ-Child.

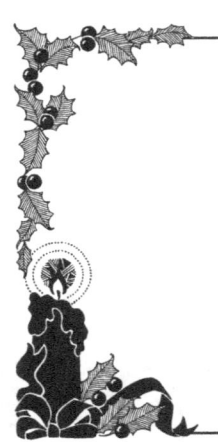

Love Came Down
By Christina Rossetti

Love came down at Christmas,
Love all lovely, Love Divine,
Love was born at Christmas,
Star and Angels gave the sign.
Worship we the Godhead,
Love Incarnate, Love Divine,

Worship we our Jesus,
But wherewith for sacred sign?
Love shall be our token,
Love be yours and love be mine,
Love to God and all men,
Love the universal sign.

Christmas Craft

Picture-Frame
By Bertha Johnston and Fanny Chapin

You will need: Cardboard
                 Raffia or Ribbon
                 Glue

Cut a circle of cardboard three and a half inches in diameter. From the center cut out a smaller circle two and a half inches in diameter. This leaves a circular cardboard frame. Wind this round and round smoothly with the raffia or ribbon. Glue another circle on the back to give a good finish, but in this second circle cut a slit in which to slide the photograph or glue the picture directly to the frame. To make it a Christmas decoration, glue a ribbon on the top. A bow at the bottom may also be added to give it a little more holiday cheer.

Variations: Make a really big one twelve or fourteen inches in diameter out of a large cardboard box and cover with large ribbon. It will almost look like a wreath. Make one of about five inches in diameter to give away as gifts.

Paper Chains
By Bertha Johnston and Fanny Chapin

You will need: Scissors
                 Paper
                 Glue

Let the little child begin by cutting strips of some bright paper or smooth wrapping paper into lengths of ½ by 3 inches (or larger if you want a bigger chain). Make a ring of one of these, putting a wee bit of glue on the under part of one end and sticking it fast to the other end by overlapping. Through this ring run another strip and glue into a similar ring, and so make a long chain of them wherewith to decorate the Christmas tree.

Remembering Those Far Away
By Howard Roscoe Driggs

Everyone likes to be remembered. In what beautiful yet inexpensive way might you remember some of your friends on Christmas? Here is a suggestion: Christmas cards and Christmas letters of your own writing and making. Such things can be bought, but we can get and give much greater pleasure by preparing them ourselves.

You have many friends to whom you would like to send something on Christmas—grandpa, grandma, father, mother, brothers, sisters, uncles, aunts, cousins, playmates. Besides these, there are other people, young and old, some of them poor, perhaps, who are seldom remembered. All of these friends would be delighted to get a Christmas greeting from you, especially if it were of your own work. You can compose a verse for your cards or write pleasant letters, adding to these a touch of Christmas by sketching or painting a bit of holly, mistletoe, or something else appropriate. Try to make such touches artistic, not gaudy.

Writing the Letters

Make the letters bright. They need not be long. Say with a happy spirit the things you wish to say. The following letter will suggest one way to do it. Do not try to imitate the letter, but rather express your own thoughts and feelings; let yours be a real letter. There are many, many ways to express our feelings and good wishes in Christmas letters.

Dear Grandma,
A Merry Christmas from your far-away little girl! I hope God will bless you with good health, good cheer, and other goodies enough to last for many years.

Your loving granddaughter,
Mary Smith

A Simple Bill of Fare for a Christmas Dinner
By Hugh Hume

All good recipe books give bills of fare for different occasions, bills of fare for grand dinners, bills of fare for little dinners; dinners to cost so much per head; to avoid too great monotony in diet, and so on. But among them all, we never saw the one which we give below. It has never been printed in any book; but it has been used in families. We are not drawing on our imagination for its items. We have sat at such dinners; we have helped prepare such dinners; we believe in such dinners; they are within everybody's means. In fact, the most marvelous thing about this bill of fare is that the dinner does not cost a cent. Ho! All ye that are hungry and thirsty, and would like so cheap a Christmas dinner, listen to this:

Christmas Dinner

First Course—GLADNESS. This must be served hot. No two housekeepers make it alike; no fixed rule can be given for it. It depends, like so many of the best things, chiefly on memory; but, strangely enough, it depends quite as much on proper forgetting as on proper remembering. Worries must be forgotten. Troubles must be forgotten. Yes, even sorrow itself must be denied and shut out. Perhaps this is not quite possible. Ah! We all have seen Christmas days on which sorrow would not leave our hearts nor our houses. But even sorrow can be compelled to look away from its sorrowing for a festival hour which is so solemnly joyous at Christ's Birthday. Memory can be filled full of other things to be remembered. No soul is entirely destitute of blessings, absolutely without comfort. Perhaps we have but one. Very well; we can think steadily of that one, if we try. But the probability is that we have more than we can count. No man has yet numbered the blessings, the mercies, the joys of God. We are all richer than we think; and if we once set ourselves to reckoning up the things of which we are glad, we shall be astonished at their number.

Entrées—LOVE, garnished with Smiles.
~GENTLENESS, with sweet-wine sauce of Laughter.
~GRACIOUS SPEECH, cooked with any fine, savory herbs, such as Frollery, which is always in season, or Pleasant Reminiscence, which no one need be without, as it keeps for years, sealed or unsealed.

Second Course—HOSPITALITY, The precise form of this also depends on individual preferences. We are not undertaking here to give exact recipes, only a bill of fare.

~In some houses Hospitality is brought on surrounded with relatives. This is very well. In others, it is dished up with dignitaries of all sorts; men and women of position and estate for whom the host has special likings or uses. This gives a fine effect to the eye, but cools quickly, and is not in the long-run satisfying.

~In a third class, best of all, it is served in simple shapes, but with a great variety of Unfortunate Persons,—such as lonely people from lodging-houses, poor people of all grades, widows and childless in their affliction. This is the kind most preferred; in fact, never abandoned by those who have tried it.

For Dessert—MIRTH, in glasses.

~GRATITUDE and FAITH beaten together and piled up in snowy shapes. These will look light if run over night in the moulds of Solid Trust and Patience.

~A dish of the bonbons GOOD CHEER and KINDLINESS with everyday mottoes; Knots and Reasons in shape of Puzzles and Answers; the whole ornamented with Apples of Gold in Pictures of Silver, of the kind mentioned in the Book of Proverbs.

This is a short and simple bill of fare. There is not a costly thing in it; not a thing which cannot be procured without difficulty.

If meat be desired, it can be added. That is another excellence about our bill of fare. It has nothing in it which makes it incongruous with the richest or the plainest tables. It is not overcrowded by the addition of roast goose and plum-pudding; it is not harmed by the addition of herring and potatoes. Nay, it can give flavor and richness to broken bits of stale bread served on a doorstep and eaten by beggars.

We might say much more about this bill of fare. We might, perhaps, confess that it has an element of the supernatural; that its origin is lost in obscurity; that, although, as we said, it has never been printed before, it has been known in all ages; that the martyrs feasted upon it; that generations of the poor, called blessed by Christ, have laid out banquets by it; that exiles and prisoners have lived on it; and the despised and forsaken and rejected in all countries have tasted it. It is also true that when any great king ate well and throve on his dinner, it was by the same magic food. The young and the free and the glad, and all rich men in costly houses, even they have not been well fed without it.

And though we have called it a Bill of Fare for a Christmas Dinner, that is only that men's eyes may be caught by its name, and that they, thinking it a specialty for festival, may learn and understand its secret, and henceforth, laying all their dinners according to its magic order, may "eat unto the Lord."

December 19

The First Christmas Tree
By Eugene Field

Once upon a time the forest was in a great commotion. Early in the evening the wise old cedars had shaken their heads ominously and predicted strange things. They had lived in the forest many, many years; but never had they seen such marvelous sights as were to be seen now in the sky, and upon the hills, and in the distant village.

"Pray tell us what you see," pleaded a little vine; "we who are not as tall as you can behold none of these wonderful things. Describe them to us, that we may enjoy them with you."

"I am filled with such amazement," said one of the cedars, "that I can hardly speak. The whole sky seems to be aflame, and the stars appear to be dancing among the clouds; angels walk down from heaven to the earth, and enter the village or talk with the shepherds upon the hills."

The vine listened in mute astonishment. Such things never before had happened. The vine trembled with excitement. Its nearest neighbor was a tiny tree, so small it scarcely ever was noticed; yet it was a very beautiful little tree, and the vines and ferns and mosses and other humble residents of the forest loved it dearly.

"How I should like to see the angels!" sighed the little tree, "and how I should like to see the stars dancing among the clouds! It must be very beautiful."

As the vine and the little tree talked of these things, the cedars watched with increasing interest the wonderful scenes over and beyond the confines of the forest. Presently they thought they heard music, and they were not mistaken, for soon the whole air was full of the sweetest harmonies ever heard upon earth.

"What beautiful music!" cried the little tree. "I wonder whence it comes."

"The angels are singing," said a cedar; "for none but angels could make such sweet music."

"But the stars are singing, too," said another cedar; "yes, and the shepherds on the hills join in the song, and what a strangely glorious song it is!"

The trees listened to the singing, but they did not understand its meaning: it seemed to be an anthem, and it was of a Child that had been born; but further than this they did not understand. The strange and glorious song continued all the night; and all that night the angels walked to and fro, and the shepherd-folk talked with the angels, and the stars danced and carolled in high heaven. And it was nearly morning when the cedars cried out, "They are coming to the forest! The angels are coming to the forest!" And, surely enough, this was true. The vine and the little tree were very terrified, and they begged their older and stronger neighbors to protect them from harm. But the cedars were too busy with their own fears to pay any heed to the faint pleadings of the humble vine and the little tree. The angels came into the forest, singing the same glorious anthem about the Child, and the stars sang in chorus with them, until every part of the woods rang with echoes of that wondrous song. There was nothing in the appearance of this angel host to inspire fear; they were clad all in white, and there were crowns upon their fair heads, and golden harps in their hands; love, hope, charity, compassion, and joy beamed from their beautiful faces, and their presence seemed to fill the forest with a divine peace. The angels came through the forest to where the little tree stood, and gathering around it, they touched it with their hands, and kissed its little branches, and sang even more sweetly than before. And their song was about the Child, the Child, the Child that had been born. Then the stars came down from the skies and danced and hung upon the branches of the tree, and they, too, sang that song,—the song of the Child. And all the other trees and the vines and the ferns and the mosses beheld in wonder; nor could they understand why all these things were being done, and why this exceeding honor should be shown the little tree.

When the morning came the angels left the forest—all but one angel, who remained behind and lingered near the little tree. Then a cedar asked: "Why do you tarry with us, holy angel?" And the angel answered: "I stay to guard this little tree, for it is sacred, and no harm shall come to it."

The little tree felt quite relieved by this assurance, and it held up its head more confidently than ever before. And how it thrived and grew, and waxed in strength and beauty! The cedars said they never had seen the like. The sun seemed to lavish its choicest rays upon the little tree, heaven dropped its sweetest dew upon it, and the winds never came to the forest that they did not forget their rude manners and linger to kiss the little tree and sing it their prettiest songs. No danger ever menaced it, no harm threatened; for the angel never slept—through the day and through the night the angel watched the little tree and protected it from all evil. Oftentimes the trees talked with the angel; but of course they understood little of what he said, for he spoke always of the Child who was to become the Master; and always when thus he talked, he caressed the little tree, and stroked its branches and leaves, and moistened them with his tears. It all was so very strange that none in the forest could understand.

So the years passed, the angel watching his blooming charge. Sometimes the beasts strayed toward the little tree and threatened to devour its tender foliage; sometimes the woodman came with his axe, intent upon hewing down the straight and comely thing; sometimes the hot, consuming breath of drought swept from the south, and sought to blight the forest and all its verdure: the angel kept them from the little tree. Serene and beautiful it grew, until now it was no longer a little tree, but the pride and glory of the forest.

One day the tree heard someone coming through the forest. Hitherto the angel had hastened to its side when men approached; but now the angel strode away and stood under the cedars yonder.

"Dear angel," cried the tree, "can you not hear the footsteps of someone approaching? Why do you leave me?"

"Have no fear," said the angel; "for He who comes is the Master."

The Master came to the tree and beheld it. He placed His hands upon its smooth trunk and branches, and the tree was thrilled with a strange and glorious delight. Then He stooped and kissed the tree, and then He turned and went away.

Many times after that the Master came to the forest, and when He came it always was to where the tree stood. Many times He rested beneath the tree and enjoyed the shade of its foliage, and listened to the music of the wind as it swept through the rustling leaves. Many times He slept there, and the tree watched over Him, and the forest was still, and all its voices were hushed. And the angel hovered near like a faithful sentinel.

Ever and anon men came with the Master to the forest, and sat with Him in the shade of the tree, and talked with Him of matters which the tree never could understand; only it heard that the talk was of love and charity and gentleness, and it saw that the Master was beloved and venerated by the others. It heard them tell of the Master's goodness and humility—how He had healed the sick and raised the dead and bestowed inestimable blessings wherever He walked. And the tree loved the Master for His beauty and His goodness; and when He came to the forest it was full of joy, but when He came not it was sad. And the other trees of the forest joined in its happiness and its sorrow, for they, too, loved the Master. And the angel always hovered near.

The Master came one night alone into the forest, and His face was pale with anguish and wet with tears, and He fell upon His knees and prayed. The tree heard Him, and all the forest was still, as if it were standing in the presence of death. And when the morning came, lo! The angel had gone.

Then there was a great confusion in the forest. There was a sound of rude voices, and a clashing of swords and staves. Strange men appeared, uttering loud oaths and cruel threats, and the tree was filled with terror. It called aloud for the angel, but the angel came not.

"Alas," cried the vine, "they have come to destroy the tree, the pride and glory of the forest!"

The forest was sorely agitated, but it was in vain. The strange men plied their axes with cruel vigor, and the tree was hewn to the ground. Its beautiful branches were cut away and cast aside, and its soft, thick foliage was strewn to the tenderer mercies of the winds.

"They are killing me!" cried the tree; "Why is not the angel here to protect me?"

But no one heard the piteous cry—none but the other trees of the forest; and they wept, and the little vine wept too.

Then the cruel men dragged the despoiled and hewn tree from the forest, and the forest saw that beauteous thing no more.

But the night wind that swept down from the City of the Great King that night to ruffle the bosom of distant Galilee, tarried in the forest awhile to say that it had seen that day a cross upraised on Calvary—the tree on which was stretched the body of the dying Master.

While Shepherds Watched
By Nahum Tate

While shepherds watched their flocks by night,
All seated on the ground.
The angel of the Lord came down,
And glory shone around.

"Fear not," said he, for mighty dread
Had seized their troubled mind;
"Glad tidings of great joy I bring
To you and all mankind."

"To you, in David's town, this day
Is born of David's line,
The Savior, who is Christ the Lord,
And this shall be the sign:
"The Heavenly Babe you there shall find
To human view displayed,
All meanly wrapped in swaddling bands,
And in a manger laid."

Thus spake the Seraph; and forthwith
Appeared a shining throng
Of angels, praising God, and thus
Addressed their joyful song.

"All glory be to God on high,
And to the earth be peace;
Good will henceforth from Heaven to men
Begin, and never cease!"

Riddles
by Melville De Lancey Landon and Mark Twain

1. What yesterday was, and what tomorrow will be. (Today)

2. I tremble with each breath of air,
And yet can heaviest burdens bear;
'Tis known that I destroyed the world,
And all things in confusion hurled;
And yet I do preserve all in it through each revolving hour and minute. (Water)

3. Pray tell us, ladies, if you can,
Who is that highly favored man.
Who, though he's married many a wife,
May be a bachelor all his life? (A clergyman)

4. I'm slain to save me—with much care and pain,
Scattered, dispersed, and gathered up again.
Withered, tho' young—most sweet, tho' unperfumed,
And carefully laid up to be consumed. (Hay)

5. A word of three syllables, seek till you find,
Which has in it twenty-six letters combined. (Alphabet)

6. Four-and-twenty white horses, now they gallop, now they canter, and now they stand still. (My teeth)

7. In spring I look happy, dressed in handsome array,
But in summer more clothing I wear;
When colder it grows, I throw off my clothes,
And in winter quite naked appear. (A tree)

8. Little Miss Netticoat, with a white petticoat and a red nose: the longer she stands the shorter she grows. (A candle)

9. Although we are but twenty-six
We change to millions too;
Surely we cannot speak a word,
Yet tell what others do. (The alphabet)

10. I bear much, devour much, and reach from pole to pole. (The sea)

11. It has two arms, two legs, and a head, like a human being, but it cannot walk or work or talk. (A doll)

12. I spend most of my life in a little wooden box. I press against its cover day and night. I want to get out. Oh, how I leap when someone opens the box! Oh, how frightened little girls and boys look when they first see me! (Jack in a box)

December 20

The Shepherd's Story
Part 1
By Washington Gladden

"Bring hither that sheepskin, Joseph, and lay it down on this bank of dry earth, under this shelving rock. The wind blows chilly from the west, but the rock will shelter us. The sky is fair and the moon is rising, and we can sit here and watch the flocks on the hillside below. Your young blood and your father's coat of skins will keep you warm for one watch, I am sure. At midnight, my son, your father, Reuben, and his brother James will take our places; for the first watch the old man and the boy will tend the sheep."

"Yes, grandfather; you shall sit in that snug corner of the rock, where you can lean back and take your comfort. I will lie here at your feet. Now and then I will run to see whether the sheep are wandering, and that will warm me, if I grow cold."

"Have you never been out on the hills at night with your father?"

"Never, grandfather. I have often begged him to let me come; but he kept saying that I must wait until I was twelve years old. On the last full moon was my birthday and today, when he returned from Bethlehem to the flocks, he brought me with him."

"So this is the lad's first night with the sheep in the fields, and the old man's last night, I fear," said the aged shepherd, sadly. "It is not often in these days that I venture out to keep the watches of the flock; but this one night of the year I have spent upon these hills these many years, and I always shall as long as I have strength to walk so far."

"Was your father, too, a shepherd?"

"Yes, and all his fathers before him for many generations. On these hills my ancestors have kept their sheep for I know not how long."

Joseph was still for a moment. His eyes wandered away over the silent hills, lit by the rising moon. His face was troubled. At length, he said gently:

"Grandfather, I heard Rabbi Eliezer saying, the other day, in the synagogue, that a shepherd's life is not a noble life. He was reading from one of the old doctors, who said: 'Let no one make his son a camel driver, a barber, a sailor, a shepherd, or a shopkeeper. They are dishonest callings.' I was angry when he read it; but I held my peace."

"You did well, my son, to hold your peace. I myself have often heard such words, of late, from the doctors in the synagogues; but it is not wise to answer them. Where they got their notions, I know not. From the Egyptians, I think, more than from the prophets. All Egyptians hate shepherds, and can never speak of them without sneering. Perhaps they have not yet forgotten how the shepherds conquered and ruled them for generations. Nevertheless, there is some reason why the calling of the shepherds should be despised. Many of them are rude and fierce men. Living out of doors so constantly makes their manners rough and their temper harsh. They are often quarrelsome. Such bloody fights as I used to see among them, at the wells in the south country, where they brought their flocks to water and each one wanted the first chance at the well, I hope you will never look upon."

"But all shepherds are not so," protested Joseph.

"No, indeed. Brave men they must be; fleet of foot and strong of limb and stout of heart; but brave men are not always quarrelsome. Many a shepherd whom I have known had a heart as pure and gentle as a child's. And the godliest men that I have known have been among them. If the shepherd has but learned to think, to commune with his own soul, he has time for thought and time for prayer. More than one with whom I have watched upon these hills knew all the Psalms of David by heart and many of the books of the prophets. The doctors in the synagogues teach only the law; the shepherds love best the Psalms and the prophets. They do not forget that King David was himself a shepherd's lad. It was upon these very hills that he kept his father's sheep. It was in that ravine over yonder, on that hillside, that he, a mere stripling, caught by the beard and killed the lion and the bear that attacked the sheep. It was on that slope, just a little to the south, that the messenger found him with his flocks when he was called home to be anointed by Samuel the prophet. When the doctors talk so contemptuously about the shepherds, I wonder if they do not remember that the great king wrote: 'The Lord is my Shepherd.' How can our calling be so mean as they say, when David, who was called from the sheep folds, praises the Eternal One himself as his Shepherd? But hark! What noise is that I hear? There is some trouble among the sheep."

"Let me run and see," answers the boy, "and I will come and bring you word."

So saying, Joseph cast off his father's shaggy coat, seized the sling in his left hand and the crook in his right and ran swiftly out to the brow of the hill. He was a strong lad, large of frame and a swift runner, and the sling in his hand was a sure weapon. The old man looked after him with pride, as he bounded over the rocks, and said to himself:

"Some evil beast, I doubt not. But the lad's heart is brave and he must learn to face dangers. I will wait a moment."

Presently the sheep came huddling round the hill in terror. The quick, faint bleat of the ewes showed that they had seen a foe. The old man arose and hurried in the direction in which the lad had disappeared. Joseph was just returning, breathless, from the ravine below.

"It was a wolf, grandfather. The sheep on this side of the ledge had seen him and were flying. Just as I reached the brow of the hill, he was creeping round the end of the ledge below, ready to spring upon a ewe that was feeding near. The first thing he knew a stone from my sling hit him, and he went howling down the hill. I think I broke his leg, for he went on three legs and I gained on him as I ran after him; but he crawled into a narrow place among the rocks in the gorge down yonder, and I could not follow him."

"Well done, my lad," said the ancient Stephanus proudly. "You will make a good shepherd. These single wolves are cowards. It is always safe to face them. When they come in packs, it is quite another thing. But this fellow will keep at a safe distance for the rest of the night, you may depend. Let us go back to our shelter and call the sheep together."

It was several minutes before Stephanus and Joseph could collect the sheep that the wolf had scattered; but at length, with the aid of the dog, who was not a very brave specimen, and who had taken to his heels when he saw the wolf coming, they succeeded in driving them into a safe neighborhood, and then, with their blood quickened by the adventure, they sat down again beneath the overhanging rock.

"You said, grandfather, that you always spent this night with the flocks in the fields. Why this night?" asked the boy.

"Do you not know, my boy, that this is the night of the year on which the Lord Christ was born?"

"Oh! Yes," answered the lad. "My father told me as we were walking hither today, but I had forgotten it. And you were with the sheep that night?"

"Aye."

"Where was it?"

"Here, on this very spot."

The boy's eyes began to grow and fill with wonder and there was a slight tremor in his voice as he hurriedly plied the aged man with his eager questions. Stephanus drew his shepherd's cloak around him, and leaned forward a little, and looked out upon the silent moonlit hills, and then up into the sky.

"How long ago was that, grandfather?"

"Just fifty years ago this night."

"And how old were you then?"

"Fourteen, and a stout boy for my age. I had been for two years in the fields with my father, and had tasted to the full the hardships and dangers of the shepherd's life."

"Who were with you on that night?"

"My father, and his brother, James, and Hosea, the son of John, a neighbor and kinsman of ours. On that year, as on this year and often, there came in the midwinter a dry and warm season between the early and the latter rain. We had driven forth our flocks from Bethlehem and were dwelling by night in the shelter of the tower on the hillside yonder, watching and sleeping two and two. My father and I were wont to keep the early watches. At midnight we would call James and Hosea, and they would watch till the morning. But that night, when the sun went down and the stars came out, we were sitting here, upon this hillside, talking of the troubles of Israel and of the promises of deliverance spoken by the prophets; and James and Hosea were asking my father questions, and he was answering them, for he was older than they, and all the people of Bethlehem reverenced him as a wise and devout man. Some even said that, if the people of Israel had not ceased to look for prophets, they would have counted him a prophet. I remember well that, when he rose in the synagogue, it seemed as if some wisdom from on high touched his lips, and he would speak with such hope and courage of the light that should yet shine in our darkness and of the help that should yet arise to Judah, that the people's faces would glow with joyful expectation."

Stephanus paused a moment and started forward, as his eye was turned toward his own shadow upon the rock, cast by the rising moon. Did the old man's figure that he saw remind him of the patriarch of whom he was talking?

Soon he went on.

"Ah! but they should have heard my father talking here by night, under the stars. It was here upon these hills where the royal shepherd used to sing, that his tongue was loosed and he spoke wonderful words. So it was that night, fifty years ago. I remember it as if it were yesterday. My father sat in this very niche, where I am sitting now; James and Hosea were on either side of him. I was lying at their feet, as you now lie at mine. Their faces kindled and the tremor of deep feeling was in their voices as they talked together; and the other two had lingered here three or four hours after the sun had set. It was not a moonlit night like this, but all the stars were out and all the winds were still.

To be continued . . .

Christmas Joy

The universal joy of Christmas is certainly wonderful. We ring the bells when princes are born, or toll a mournful dirge when great men pass away. Nations have their red-letter days, their carnivals and festivals, but once in the year and only once, the whole world stands still to celebrate the advent of a life. Only Jesus of Nazareth claims this world-wide, undying remembrance. You cannot cut Christmas out of the Calendar, nor out of the heart of the world.

Christmas Carols

Sing the two Christmas Carols together as a family. Discuss what the songs mean.

I Heard the Bells on Christmas Day

Henry W. Longfellow, 1863 — J. Baptiste Calkin, 1872

1. I heard the bells on Christ-mas day Their old fa-mil-iar car-ols play,
2. I thought how, as the day had come, The bel-fries of all Chris-ten-dom
3. And in de-spair I bowed my head: 'There is no peace on earth,' I said,
4. Then pealed the bells more loud and deep: 'God is not dead, nor doth he sleep;
5. Till, ring-ing, sing-ing on its way, The world re-volved from night to day,

And wild and sweet the words re-peat Of peace on earth, good-will to men.
Had rolled along the un-bro-ken song Of peace on earth, good-will to men,
'For hate is strong, and mocks the song Of peace on earth, good-will to men.'
The wrong shall fail, the right pre-vail, With peace on earth, good-will to men':
A voice, a chime, a chant sub-lime, Of peace on earth, good-will to men! A-men.

Countdown to Christmas — Amy Puetz Fox

December 21

The Shepherd's Story
Part 2
By Washington Gladden

Suddenly I saw my father rise to his feet. Then the other men sprang up, with astonishment and wonder upon their faces. It had grown light all at once, lighter than the brightest moon; and as I turned my face in the direction in which the others were looking, I saw, standing there upon that level place, a figure majestic and beautiful beyond all the power of words to tell."

"Were you not afraid, grandfather?"

"Indeed, I was, my boy. My heart stopped beating. The others were standing, but I had no power to rise. I lay there motionless upon the earth. My eyes were fixed upon that wonderful face; upon those clear, shining eyes; upon that brow that seemed to beam with the purity of the soul within. It was not a smile with which that face was lighted. It was something too noble and exalted to call by that name. It was a look that told of power and peace, of joy and triumph."

"Did you know that it was an angel?"

"I knew not anything. I only knew that what I saw was glorious, too glorious for mortal eyes to look upon. Yet, while I gazed, and in far less time than I have now taken to tell you of what I saw, the terribleness of the look began to disappear, the sweetness and grace of the soul shone forth, and I had almost ceased to tremble before the angel opened his mouth. And when he spoke, his voice, clearer than any trumpet and sweeter than any lute, charmed away all my fears."

"'Be not afraid' he said, 'for behold I bring you good tidings of great joy which shall be to all people. For there is born to you this day, in the City of David, a Savior, which is Messiah, the King. And this is the sign unto you. Ye shall find a babe wrapped in swaddling clothes and lying in a manger.'

"Oh! that voice, my boy! It makes my heart beat now to remember its sweetness. It seemed to carry these words into our innermost hearts; to print them on our memory, so that we never could forget one syllable of what he said. And then, before we had time to make reply, he turned aside a little and lifted his face toward heaven, and, in a tone far louder than that in which he had spoken to us, but yet so sweet that it did not startle us at all, came forth from his lips the first strain of the great song:

"'Glory to God in the highest!'

"When he had uttered that, he paused a moment, and the echoes, one after another, from hills that were near and hills that were far away, came flying home to us; so that I knew for once what the prophet meant when he said that all the mountains and the hills should break forth into singing. But before the echoes had all faded we began to hear other voices above our heads, a great chorus, taking up the strain that the angel first had sung. At first it seemed dim and far away; but gradually it came nearer, and filled all the air, filled all the earth, filled all our souls with a most entrancing sweetness. Glory to God in the highest!—That was the grandest part. It seemed as though there could be no place so high that the strain would not mount up to it, and no place so happy that the voice would not make it thrill with new gladness. But then came the softer tones, less grand, but even sweeter: 'Peace on earth; good will to men.'

"Oh! My boy, if you had heard that music as I did, you would not wonder when I tell you that it has been hard for me to wait here, in the midst of the dreary noises of earth, for fifty years before hearing it again. But earth that night was as musical as heaven. You should have heard the echoes that came back, when the angels' chorus ceased, from all these mountains and all these little hills on every side. There is music enough even in this world, if one can only call it forth; chords divine that will vibrate with wonderful harmony. It only needs an angel's hand to touch the trembling strings."

"Did you see the choir of angels overhead, grandfather?"

"Nay, I saw nothing. The brightness was too dazzling for mortal eyes. We all stood there, with downcast eyes, listening spellbound to the wonderful melody, until the chorus ceased, and the echoes, one after another, died away, and the glory faded out of the sky and the stars came back again, and no sound was heard but the faint voice of a young lamb, calling for its mother.

"The first to break the silence was my father. 'Come,' he said, in a solemn voice. 'Let us go at once to Bethlehem, and see this thing which is come to pass, which the Lord hath made known unto us.' So the sheep were quietly gathered into the fold at the tower, and we hastened to Bethlehem. Never shall I forget that journey by night. We spake not many words, as we traveled swiftly the twenty furlongs; talk seemed altogether tame; but now and then my father broke forth in a song, and the others joined in the chorus. We were not so spent with running but that we could find voice for singing; and such words as these of the prophet were the only ones that could give voice to our swelling hearts:

"*'Sing, O heavens; and be joyful, O earth;*
And break forth into singing, O mountains;
For the Lord hath comforted His people,
And will have mercy on His afflicted.

"*'How beautiful upon the mountains*
Are the feet of Him that bringeth good tidings,
That publisheth peace,
That bringeth good tidings of good,
That publisheth salvation.'

"It was midnight when we climbed the hill to the little city of Bethlehem; the constellation Cesil, called by the Greeks Orion, was just setting in the west. We knew not whither to go. We had only the sign of the angel by which we should know the infant Messiah. He was a babe of one day. He was lying in a manger.

"'Let us go to the inn Chimham,' said my father. 'It stands on the very spot where King David was born. Peradvanture we shall find him there.'

"Over the entrance to the court of the inn a lantern was swinging from a rope stretched across from post to post. Guided by its light, we entered, and found the courtyard full of beasts of burden, showing that the inn was crowded with travelers. In the arched shelter of the hostelry as many as could find room were lying; some who could not sleep were sitting up and waiting drearily for the morning. Two aged women near the entrance, were talking in a low tone.

"'Peace be unto you!' said my father.

"'The Lord be gracious unto thee,' answered the oldest woman, in a solemn voice, as she looked upon my father's white beard; 'but,' she quickly added, 'there is scanty cheer in this place for late comers.'

"'We seek not lodging,' said my father; 'but know you whether among these guests is an infant born this day?'

"'Verily there is,' answered the aged dame; 'a man-child more beautiful than any my eyes have ever beheld. He is lying in a manger there in the cave that serves for stable.'

"We hastened to the mouth of the cave, and there beheld our King. The oxen and the donkeys were lying near, and a strong man, with a grave and benignant face, was leaning on his staff above the manger. A beautiful young mother lay close beside it, her cheek resting on her hands, that were clasped over the edge of the rock-hewn crib. Into this a little straw had been thrown, and over it a purple robe had been cast, whereon the infant lay. A lamp, set upon a projection of the wall of the cave, burned brightly near. The great eyes of the wonderful child were wandering about the room; his hand touched his mother's lips. I waited to hear him open his mouth and speak.

"There was a moment of silence after we entered the cave. My father broke it with his salutation:

"'Hail, thou blessed among women!' he cried. 'This child of thine is a Prince and a Savior.'

"And then we all bowed low upon our faces before him and worshiped him with praise and gladness.

"The two aged women, with whom we had spoken, had followed us to the door of the stable, and, seeing us worshiping there, had run to call others who were awake in the inn, so that when we arose quite a company were standing at the door, or just within, gazing upon the King in his beauty and listening to our thanksgiving with great wonder.

"Then my father told them all the things that we had heard and seen—the message of the angel, the song in the air, the glory of the Lord that had appeared to us—and how we had quickly come to Bethlehem, and had found things as the angel had told us. 'And it is even,' he cried, 'as the prophet himself hath spoken: "Thou Bethlehem Ephratah, though thou be little among the thousands of Judah, yet out of thee shall he come forth unto me that is to be ruler in Israel, whose going forth hast been of old; even from everlasting."'

"All that heard were full of astonishment—all save the mother. I saw no wonder on her face; the great things that my father told caused her no astonishment; she listened with a quiet and solemn joy, like one who was saying in her heart: 'I knew it all before.'

"When my father had finished speaking, we all bowed low again before the young child; and the mother lifted him in her arms and placed his cheek against her own, smiling graciously on us, but uttering no word. And we came forth from the stable and stood again beneath the stars in the courtyard of the inn. By this time many of the travelers were awake, and an eager company had gathered around us, all of whom desired to be told of the sign that had been shown to us. To one and another we rehearsed our story, lingering long to make known the good tidings, until the morning star appeared and the dawn began to kindle over the eastern hills. Then we hastened to our own homes in the city, and told our kindred what had happened unto us. In the early morning we came back again unto our pastures and our flocks, rejoicing to stand again in the place where the glory of God had shone and the music of heaven had filled the air."

Stephanus paused, his face all-aglow with the tale that he had been telling. His eyes swept again the circuit of the moonlit hills and were lifted reverently up to the sky.

"Did you ever see the Lord Christ after that?" asked Joseph.

"Once only. My father and I were at Jerusalem at the Passover. It was the year before my father died, seventeen years ago; it was the same week on which our Lord was crucified. My father was then an aged man—fourscore and five years old. Our tent was pitched on the slope of the Mount of Olives, near the Bethany road. While we sat there one morning, a great noise of shouting was heard, and presently we saw one riding on an donkey, followed by a great company, crying 'Hosanna!' As we drew nearer, we heard them say that it was Jesus of Nazareth; and, when we saw His face, we knew that it was He, by the wonderful eyes, though it was the face of a bearded man, and not of an infant, and was very pale and sad. As He drew near to our tent, the city came full into His view, with its gilded roofs and marble pinnacles, blazing under the morning sun. Suddenly He paused in the way, and we heard Him weeping aloud, though we could not hear His words of lamentation. The multitude halted, too, when we did; and the cheering ceased, and some of those who stood nearest Him wept also, though no one seemed to know what had caused His grief. But soon they went on again, and before they reached the foot of the hill another multitude met them, coming forth from the city, and we heard their shouts of 'Hosanna in the Highest!' as they entered the gate of Jerusalem."

"What said your father when he saw all this?" queried Joseph.

"He said but little. There was a shadow on his face, yet he spoke cheerfully. 'I cannot understand it,' he murmured. 'They are trying to make Him King of the Jews; but King He will not be, at least not in their fashion. Yet in some way I know He will be Prince and Deliverer. I cannot understand, I will wait.'"

"Were you not in Jerusalem when He was put to death?"

"No. My father was frail and ill and we had hastened home to Bethlehem. News of His death on the cross had only just reached us when another messenger came to tell us that the sepulcher in which He had been laid was empty; that He had risen from the dead.

"My father's eyes kindled when he heard this message. He cast aside his staff and stood firm on his feet. His voice, when he spoke, rang out like a trumpet. 'Blessed be the Lord God of Israel!' he cried. It is thus that He redeemeth His people. This Jesus is not to be the Captain of our armies, but the Savior of our souls. His kingdom is the kingdom of righteousness, and therefore it is that the prophet hath said: "Of the increase of His government and peace there shall be no end."

"Always after that, words of the prophet concerning the Messiah kept coming back to my father; and once and again he cried out: 'Truly, this Jesus was the Son of God, the true King of Israel!' As the months wore on, his words were more and more of the crucified and risen Lord, and he dwelt in a great peace. At length, when the flocks were led forth to the midwinter pasturage, he begged to go with me. It was on this very day that we came, the same day of the year on which the Lord was born. He was feeble and tottered as he walked; but he leaned on my arm and we came slowly. In the evening he said: 'Let me go, my son, and sit once more under the great rock.' I wrapped him in my coat of skins, and sat here where I sit now and where he was sitting when the angel came. We talked here long, under the stars, that night, of Him whom we had learned to love as Master and Lord, of the works that He had done and the words that He had spoken, as His disciples had told of them. We had been silent for a few moments, when I looked up, and saw that his head had fallen backward against the rock wall. I sprang to him. His eyes were shut, but his lips were moving. I put my ear to his mouth, and heard him say only: 'Peace—on—earth good will'—they were his last words. He had gone beyond our starlight, into the country where the light always shines—the glory that fell that night, fifty years ago, upon these hills of Bethlehem."

Stephanus was silent and Joseph's eyes were full of tears. At length the old man rose.

"Come, my son," he said. "Cesil is in the south; it is midnight; let us call your father and his brother. The old man and the boy have kept their watch, and it is now time for rest."

The Birth of Christ
By Alfred Tennyson

The time draws near the birth of Christ;
The moon is hid—the night is still;
The Christmas bells from hill to hill
Answer each other in the mist.

Four voices of four hamlets round,
From far and near, on mead and moor,
Swell out and fail, as if a door
Were shut between me and the sound.

Each voice four changes on the wind,
That now dilate and now decrease,
Peace and good-will, good-will and peace,
Peace and good-will to all mankind.

Rise, happy morn! Rise, holy morn!
Draw forth the cheerful day from night;
O Father! Touch the east, and light
The light that shone when hope was born!

Christmas Cooking

Christmas Cookies

3 cups all-purpose flour
½ teaspoon baking powder
1/8 teaspoon salt
½ cup sugar
1 egg
2 teaspoons vanilla
1 cup butter or margarine

Mix flour, baking powder, and salt. Use a mixer to cream butter and sugar together thoroughly. Add egg and vanilla. Beat until fluffy. Gradually stir in sifted dry ingredients until well-blended. Roll small amount of dough 1/8 inch thick on lightly-floured board. Cut with cookie cutters. Bake on ungreased cookie sheet at 350° until delicately browned, 10 to 12 minutes.

Once the cookies are cool decorate with frosting. You can use store bought frosting or make your own.

Frosting

Add 2 tablespoons hot water to one cup powdered sugar. Add food coloring. Pour on the cookies as desired.

Gingerbread Men Cookies

1/3 cup shortening
1/3 cup brown sugar
1 egg
1 cup molasses
1¾ cups flour

½ teaspoon soda
1 teaspoon ginger
½ teaspoon nutmeg
½ teaspoon cinnamon
½ teaspoon salt

Mix the shortening, sugar, molasses, and eggs well; mix all the dry ingredients and sift into the first mixture. Add a little more flour if necessary. Roll to ¼ inch in thickness, flour if necessary, cut into fancy shapes as liked. Bake on greased cookie sheet at 350° until delicately browned, 8 to 10 minutes. If "gingerbread men" are made, currants or raisins may be used for the eyes and nose.

December 22

The Coming Messiah
From the Bible

Feel free to read these passages in a contemporary version if it would be easier for the children to understand. ~Amy

Hosea 11:1

When Israel was a child, then I loved him, and called my son out of Egypt.

Micah 5:2-5a

But thou, Bethlehem Ephratah, though thou be little among the thousands of Judah, yet out of thee shall he come forth unto me that is to be ruler in Israel; whose goings forth have been from of old, from everlasting. Therefore will he give them up, until the time that she which travaileth hath brought forth: then the remnant of his brethren shall return unto the children of Israel. And he shall stand and feed in the strength of the LORD, in the majesty of the name of the LORD his God; and they shall abide: for now shall he be great unto the ends of the earth. And this man shall be the peace.

Jeremiah 31:15

Thus saith the LORD; A voice was heard in Ramah, lamentation, and bitter weeping; Rachel weeping for her children refused to be comforted for her children, because they were not.

Jeremiah 23:5-8

Behold, the days come, saith the LORD, that I will raise unto David a righteous Branch, and a King shall reign and prosper, and shall execute judgment and justice in the earth. In his days Judah shall be saved, and Israel shall dwell safely: and this is his name whereby he shall be called, THE LORD OUR RIGHTEOUSNESS. Therefore, behold, the days come, saith the LORD, that they shall no more say, The LORD liveth, which brought up the children of Israel out of the land of Egypt; But, The LORD liveth, which brought up and which led the seed of the house of Israel out of the north country, and from all countries whither I had driven them; and they shall dwell in their own land.

Isaiah 7:14

Therefore the Lord himself shall give you a sign; Behold, a virgin shall conceive, and bear a son, and shall call his name Immanuel.

Isaiah 9:2-7

The people that walked in darkness have seen a great light: they that dwell in the land of the shadow of death, upon them hath the light shined. Thou hast multiplied the nation, and not increased the joy: they joy before thee according to the joy in harvest, and as men rejoice when they divide the spoil. For thou hast broken the yoke of his burden, and the staff of his shoulder, the rod of his oppressor, as in the day of Midian. For every battle of the warrior is with confused noise, and garments rolled in blood; but this shall be with burning and fuel of fire. For unto us a child is born, unto us a son is given: and the government shall be upon his shoulder: and his name shall be called Wonderful, Counsellor, The mighty God, The everlasting Father, The Prince of Peace. Of the increase of his government and peace there shall be no end, upon the throne of David, and upon his kingdom, to order it, and to establish it with judgment and with justice from henceforth even for ever. The zeal of the LORD of hosts will perform this.

Christmas Day
By Christina Rossetti

A baby is a harmless thing,
And wins our hearts with one accord,
And Flower of babies was their King
Jesus Christ our Lord:
Lily of lilies He
Upon His Mother's knee;
Rose of roses, soon to be
Crowned with thorns on leafless tree.
A lamb is innocent and mild
And merry on the soft green sod,
And Jesus Christ the Undented,
Is the Lamb of God:
Only spotless He
Upon His Mother's knee;
White and ruddy, soon to be,
Sacrificed for you and me.
Nay, lamb is not so sweet a word,
Nor lily half so pure a name;
Another name our hearts hath stirred
Kindling them to flame:
"Jesus" certainly
Is music and melody,
Heart with heart in harmony
Carol we and worship we.

Christmas Games

How, When, and Where by Laura Valentine

Charles Dickens mentions this game in his book A Christmas Carol. Scrooge's nephew Fred and his friends enjoyed this game at Christmas time. ~Amy

The players are seated in a line or circle. One is chosen to ask the questions; he or she goes out of the room and closes the door, that he or she may not hear the word chosen. The players then select a word; if it has many meanings, so much the better.

When they have fixed on it, they call the one who is outside the door into the room. He or she goes round the circle, asking first, "Why do you like it?" then he or she walks round a second time, asking, "When do you like it?" and a third time, asking, "Where do you like it?" From the answers received he or she guesses the word. The person is allowed to guess three times; if wrong all three times, he or she losses and must go out of the room again.

Example:

Helen goes out of the room, and returns to guess. She asks Ada, "Why do you like it?"

Ada: Because it is pretty.

Helen: Why do you like it, Jessy?

Jessy: Because it is so silent.

Helen: Why do you like it, Jane?

Jane: Because mamma gave it to me.

Helen: Why do you like it, Edith?

Emm: Because it pleases Baby.

Helen asks, "When do you like it?"

Ada: When it is made of wax.

Jessy: When it is made of china.

Jane: When it is made of wood.

Edith: When it is made of rags.

Helen: Where do you like it?

Ada: In the playroom.

Jessy: In my lap.

Jane: In a cradle.

Edith: In a shop.

Helen: I can guess it, because I think only a DOLL would be made of wax, china, wood, and rags.

Edith: Yes; you are right. When did you guess what it was?

Helen: When Ada said, "Made of wax."

Edith: Then, as Ada told what it was, it is her turn to leave the room.

Contradiction by Laura Valentine

Four players hold a handkerchief by its corners. One stands by them who commands their movements. But the game is Contradiction; therefore when she says, "Hold fast!" they drop the handkerchief; when she cries, "Let go!" they must hold it tightly. For obedience to the order given the person must trade places with the one who gives the commands.

December 23

Birth of Jesus
Matthew 1:17-2:23

So all the generations from Abraham to David are fourteen generations; and from David until the carrying away into Babylon are fourteen generations; and from the carrying away into Babylon unto Christ are fourteen generations.

Now the birth of Jesus Christ was on this wise: When as his mother Mary was espoused to Joseph, before they came together, she was found with child of the Holy Ghost. Then Joseph her husband, being a just man, and not willing to make her a publick example, was minded to put her away privily. But while he thought on these things, behold, the angel of the Lord appeared unto him in a dream, saying, Joseph, thou son of David, fear not to take unto thee Mary thy wife: for that which is conceived in her is of the Holy Ghost. And she shall bring forth a son, and thou shalt call his name JESUS: for he shall save his people from their sins. Now all this was done, that it might be fulfilled which was spoken of the Lord by the prophet, saying, Behold, a virgin shall be with child, and shall bring forth a son, and they shall call his name Emmanuel, which being interpreted is, God with us. Then Joseph being raised from sleep did as the angel of the Lord had bidden him, and took unto him his wife: And knew her not till she had brought forth her firstborn son: and he called his name JESUS. Now when Jesus was born in Bethlehem of Judaea in the days of Herod the king, behold, there came wise men from the east to Jerusalem, Saying, Where is he that is born King of the Jews for we have seen his star in the east, and are come to worship him. When Herod the king had heard these things, he was troubled, and all Jerusalem with him. And when he had gathered all the chief priests and scribes of the people together, he demanded of them where Christ should be born. And they said unto him, In Bethlehem of Judaea: for thus it is written by the prophet, And thou Bethlehem, in the land of Juda, art not the least among the princes of Judah: for out of thee shall come a Governor, that shall rule my people Israel. Then Herod, when he had privily called the wise men, enquired of them diligently what time the star appeared. And he sent them to Bethlehem, and said, Go and search diligently for the young child; and when ye have found him, bring me word again, that I may come and worship him also. When they had heard the king, they departed; and, lo, the star, which they saw in the east, went before them, till it came and stood over where the young child was. When they saw the star, they rejoiced with exceeding great joy.

And when they were come into the house, they saw the young child with Mary his mother, and fell down, and worshipped him: and when they had opened their treasures, they presented unto him gifts; gold, and frankincense, and myrrh. And being warned of God in a dream that they should not return to Herod, they departed into their own country another way. And when they were departed, behold, the angel of the Lord appeareth to Joseph in a dream, saying, Arise, and take the young child and his mother, and flee into Egypt, and be thou there until I bring thee word: for Herod will seek the young child to destroy him. When he arose, he took the young child and his mother by night, and departed into Egypt: And was there until the death of Herod: that it might be fulfilled which was spoken of the Lord by the prophet, saying, Out of Egypt have I called my son.

Then Herod, when he saw that he was mocked of the wise men, was exceeding wroth, and sent forth, and slew all the children that were in Bethlehem, and in all the coasts thereof, from two years old and under, according to the time which he had diligently enquired of the wise men. Then was fulfilled that which was spoken by Jeremy the prophet, saying, In Rama was there a voice heard, lamentation, and weeping, and great mourning, Rachel weeping for her children, and would not be comforted, because they are not.

But when Herod was dead, behold, an angel of the Lord appeareth in a dream to Joseph in Egypt, Saying, Arise, and take the young child and his mother, and go into the land of Israel: for they are dead which sought the young child's life. And he arose, and took the young child and his mother, and came into the land of Israel. But when he heard that Archelaus did reign in Judaea in the room of his father Herod, he was afraid to go thither: notwithstanding, being warned of God in a dream, he turned aside into the parts of Galilee: And he came and dwelt in a city called Nazareth: that it might be fulfilled which was spoken by the prophets, He shall be called a Nazarene.

The Christmas Spirit

By Hugh Hume

The spirit of Christmas is one of the best gifts that Christianity has bestowed upon us. It speaks in a language that is foreign to none and native to all—the language of fellowship and sisterhood. It should be cultivated to the end that instead of manifesting itself but once a year, it would become a beautiful flower of perennial bloom. It would be a fine old world, indeed, if we made the Christian spirit the sentiment of everyday life.

Christmas Craft

Christmas Carol Wall Hanging
By Amy Puetz Fox

You will need:
8"x10" piece of cardboard
Old Christmas Cards
Glue Stick
Card Stock

1. Cut an 8"x10" piece off a cardboard box. Decide which Christmas Carol you would like to use for your wall hanging. Gather some old Christmas cards and find six to eight that have a similar color scheme and theme. For example, if you choose "We Three Kings," use Christmas cards that have pictures of the wise men on them.

2. Copy the Carol you want. There are several of them in this book that you could use. You can copy it and then reduce the size on a copy machine. The songs look very nice printed on resume type paper.

3. Now that you have a song and Christmas cards, it's time to put it all together. Lay the cards on the cardboard until you find the look you want and then glue them to the cardboard. Now take a page of colored card stock and cut it slightly bigger than the song. I ripped the edges of mine to give it a ragged look, but you could cut it with decorative scissors or just straight scissors. Glue the song to the card stock and then glue the card stock to the cardboard.

4. Once the glue has dried, the wall hanging can be placed in a picture frame or just used by itself.

Other ideas:
There are lots of different ways you can use this general idea. You could put many mismatched colored cards together and then put a thin coat of gold or silver craft paint over it (pictures below). Instead of a song you could use a Christmas card for the center of the wall hanging. You could make three complementing pictures, such as two 5"x7" and one 8"x10". These make great gifts!

December 24

The Christmas Story
Luke 1

Forasmuch as many have taken in hand to set forth in order a declaration of those things which are most surely believed among us, Even as they delivered them unto us, which from the beginning were eyewitnesses, and ministers of the word; It seemed good to me also, having had perfect understanding of all things from the very first, to write unto thee in order, most excellent Theophilus, That thou mightest know the certainty of those things, wherein thou hast been instructed.

There was in the days of Herod, the king of Judaea, a certain priest named Zacharias, of the course of Abia: and his wife was of the daughters of Aaron, and her name was Elisabeth. And they were both righteous before God, walking in all the commandments and ordinances of the Lord blameless. And they had no child, because that Elisabeth was barren, and they both were now well stricken in years. And it came to pass, that while he executed the priest's office before God in the order of his course, According to the custom of the priest's office, his lot was to burn incense when he went into the temple of the Lord. And the whole multitude of the people were praying without at the time of incense. And there appeared unto him an angel of the Lord standing on the right side of the altar of incense. And when Zacharias saw him, he was troubled, and fear fell upon him. But the angel said unto him, Fear not, Zacharias: for thy prayer is heard; and thy wife Elisabeth shall bear thee a son, and thou shalt call his name John. And thou shalt have joy and gladness; and many shall rejoice at his birth. For he shall be great in the sight of the Lord, and shall drink neither wine nor strong drink; and he shall be filled with the Holy Ghost, even from his mother's womb. And many of the children of Israel shall he turn to the Lord their God. And he shall go before him in the spirit and power of Elias, to turn the hearts of the fathers to the children, and the disobedient to the wisdom of the just; to make ready a people prepared for the Lord. And Zacharias said unto the angel, Whereby shall I know this for I am an old man, and my wife well stricken in years. And the angel answering said unto him, I am Gabriel, that stand in the presence of God; and am sent to speak unto thee, and to shew thee these glad tidings. And, behold, thou shalt be dumb, and not able to speak, until the day that these things shall be performed, because thou believest not my words, which shall be fulfilled in their season. And the people waited for Zacharias, and marvelled that he tarried so long in the temple. And when he came out, he could not speak unto them: and they perceived that he had seen a vision in the temple: for he beckoned unto them, and remained speechless. And it came to pass, that, as soon as the days of his ministration were accomplished, he departed to his own house. And after those days his wife Elisabeth conceived, and hid herself five months, saying, Thus hath the Lord dealt with me in the days wherein he looked on me, to take away my reproach among men.

And in the sixth month the angel Gabriel was sent from God unto a city of Galilee, named Nazareth, To a virgin espoused to a man whose name was Joseph, of the house of David; and the virgin's name was Mary. And the angel came in unto her, and said, Hail, thou that art highly favoured, the Lord is with thee: blessed art thou among women. And when she saw him, she was troubled at his saying, and cast in her mind what manner of salutation this should be. And the angel said unto her, Fear not, Mary: for thou hast found favour with God. And, behold, thou shalt conceive in thy womb, and bring forth a son, and shalt call his name JESUS. He shall be great, and shall be called the Son of the Highest: and the Lord God shall give unto him the throne of his father David: And he shall reign over the house of Jacob for ever; and of his kingdom there shall be no end. Then said Mary unto the angel, How shall this be, seeing I know not a man? And the angel answered and said unto her, The Holy Ghost shall come upon thee, and the power of the Highest shall overshadow thee: therefore also that holy thing which shall be born of thee shall be called the Son of God. And, behold, thy cousin Elisabeth, she hath also conceived a son in her old age: and this is the sixth month with her, who was called barren. For with God nothing shall be impossible. And Mary said, Behold the handmaid of the Lord; be it unto me according to thy word. And the angel departed from her. And Mary arose in those days, and went into the hill country with haste, into a city of Juda; And entered into the house of Zacharias, and saluted Elisabeth. And it came to pass, that, when Elisabeth heard the salutation of Mary, the babe leaped in her womb; and Elisabeth was filled with the Holy Ghost: And she spake out with a loud voice, and said, Blessed art thou among women, and blessed is the fruit of thy womb. And whence is this to me, that the mother of my Lord should come to me? For, lo, as soon as the voice of thy salutation sounded in mine ears, the babe leaped in my womb for joy. And blessed is she that believed: for there shall be a performance of those things which were told her from the Lord. And Mary said, My soul doth magnify the Lord, And my spirit hath rejoiced in God my Saviour. For he hath regarded the low estate of his handmaiden: for, behold, from henceforth all generations shall call me blessed. For he that is mighty hath done to me great things; and holy is his name. And his mercy is on them that fear him from generation to generation. He hath shewed strength with his arm; he hath scattered the proud in the imagination of their hearts. He hath put down the mighty from their seats, and exalted them of low degree. He hath filled the hungry with good things; and the rich he hath sent empty away. He hath holpen his servant Israel, in remembrance of his mercy; As he spake to our fathers, to Abraham, and to his seed for ever. And Mary abode with her about three months, and returned to her own house.

Now Elisabeth's full time came that she should be delivered; and she brought forth a son. And her neighbours and her cousins heard how the Lord had shewed great mercy upon her; and they rejoiced with her. And it came to pass, that on the eighth day they came to circumcise the child; and they called him Zacharias, after the name of his father. And his mother answered and said, Not so; but he shall be called John. And they said unto her, There is none of thy kindred that is called by this name. And they made signs to his father, how he would have him called. And he asked for a writing table, and wrote, saying, His name is John. And they marvelled all. And his mouth was opened immediately, and his tongue loosed, and he spake, and praised God. And fear came on all that dwelt round about them: and all these sayings were noised abroad throughout all the hill country of Judaea. And all they that heard them laid them up in their hearts, saying, What manner of child shall this be! And the hand of the Lord was with him.

And his father Zacharias was filled with the Holy Ghost, and prophesied, saying, Blessed be the Lord God of Israel; for he hath visited and redeemed his people, And hath raised up an horn of salvation for us in the house of his servant David; As he spake by the mouth of his holy prophets, which have been since the world began: That we should be saved from our enemies, and from the hand of all that hate us; To perform the mercy promised to our fathers, and to remember his holy covenant; The oath which he sware to our father Abraham, That he would grant unto us, that we being delivered out of the hand of our enemies might serve him without fear, In holiness and righteousness before him, all the days of our life. And thou, child, shalt be called the prophet of the Highest: for thou shalt go before the face of the Lord to prepare his ways; To give knowledge of salvation unto his people by the remission of their sins, Through the tender mercy of our God; whereby the dayspring from on high hath visited us, To give light to them that sit in darkness and in the shadow of death, to guide our feet into the way of peace. And the child grew, and waxed strong in spirit, and was in the deserts till the day of his shewing unto Israel.

Christmas Quiz

Who Said It? by Amy Puetz Fox

Match the line on the left with the person who said it on the right.

1) God bless us every one.

2) Mankind was my business. The common welfare was my business; charity, mercy, forbearance, and benevolence, were all, my business.

3) What right have you to be merry? What reason have you to be merry? You're poor enough.

4) One dollar and eighty-seven cents. That was all. And sixty cents of it was in pennies. Pennies saved one and two at a time by bulldozing the grocer and the vegetable man and the butcher until one's cheeks burned with the silent imputation of parsimony that such close dealing implied. Three times Della counted it. One dollar and eighty-seven cents. And the next day would be Christmas.

5) Come, then, what right have you to be dismal? What reason have you to be morose? You're rich enough.

6) And it was always said of him (Scrooge), that he knew how to keep Christmas well, if any man alive possessed the knowledge.

7) Christmas won't be Christmas without any presents.

8) Fear not for behold I bring you good tidings of great joy.

9) Glory to God in the highest and on earth good will to all men.

A) O. Henry, *Gift of the Magi*

B) Jo March

C) Ebenezer Scrooge

D) Song the angels sang

E) Fred, Scrooge's nephew

F) Charles Dickens, *A Christmas Carol*

G) Jacob Marley

H) Tiny Tim

I) The Angel

Answers
1-H, 2-G, 3-C, 4-A, 5-E, 6-F, 7-B, 8-I, 9-D

December 25

Christ is Born
Luke 2

And it came to pass in those days, that there went out a decree from Caesar Augustus, that all the world should be taxed. (And this taxing was first made when Cyrenius was governor of Syria.) And all went to be taxed, every one into his own city. And Joseph also went up from Galilee, out of the city of Nazareth, into Judaea, unto the city of David, which is called Bethlehem; (because he was of the house and lineage of David:) To be taxed with Mary his espoused wife, being great with child. And so it was, that, while they were there, the days were accomplished that she should be delivered. And she brought forth her firstborn son, and wrapped him in swaddling clothes, and laid him in a manger; because there was no room for them in the inn.

And there were in the same country shepherds abiding in the field, keeping watch over their flock by night. And, lo, the angel of the Lord came upon them, and the glory of the Lord shone round about them: and they were sore afraid. And the angel said unto them, Fear not: for, behold, I bring you good tidings of great joy, which shall be to all people. For unto you is born this day in the city of David a Saviour, which is Christ the Lord. And this shall be a sign unto you; Ye shall find the babe wrapped in swaddling clothes, lying in a manger. And suddenly there was with the angel a multitude of the heavenly host praising God, and saying, Glory to God in the highest, and on earth peace, good will toward men. And it came to pass, as the angels were gone away from them into heaven, the shepherds said one to another, Let us now go even unto Bethlehem, and see this thing which is come to pass, which the Lord hath made known unto us. And they came with haste, and found Mary, and Joseph, and the babe lying in a manger. And when they had seen it, they made known abroad the saying which was told them concerning this child. And all they that heard it wondered at those things which were told them by the shepherds. But Mary kept all these things, and pondered them in her heart. And the shepherds returned, glorifying and praising God for all the things that they had heard and seen, as it was told unto them.

And when eight days were accomplished for the circumcising of the child, his name was called JESUS, which was so named of the angel before he was conceived in the womb. And when the days of her purification according to the law of Moses were accomplished, they brought him to Jerusalem, to present him to the Lord; (As it is written in the law of the Lord, Every male that openeth the womb shall be called holy to the Lord;) And to offer a sacrifice according to that which is said in the law of the Lord, A pair of turtledoves, or two young pigeons.

And, behold, there was a man in Jerusalem, whose name was Simeon; and the same man was just and devout, waiting for the consolation of Israel: and the Holy Ghost was upon him. And it was revealed unto him by the Holy Ghost, that he should not see death, before he had seen the Lord's Christ. And he came by the Spirit into the temple: and when the parents brought in the child Jesus, to do for him after the custom of the law, Then took he him up in his arms, and blessed God, and said, Lord, now lettest thou thy servant depart in peace, according to thy word: For mine eyes have seen thy salvation, Which thou hast prepared before the face of all people; A light to lighten the Gentiles, and the glory of thy people Israel. And Joseph and his mother marvelled at those things which were spoken of him. And Simeon blessed them, and said unto Mary his mother, Behold, this child is set for the fall and rising again of many in Israel; and for a sign which shall be spoken against; (Yea, a sword shall pierce through thy own soul also,) that the thoughts of many hearts may be revealed. And there was one Anna, a prophetess, the daughter of Phanuel, of the tribe of Aser: she was of a great age, and had lived with an husband seven years from her virginity; And she was a widow of about fourscore and four years, which departed not from the temple, but served God with fastings and prayers night and day. And she coming in that instant gave thanks likewise unto the Lord, and spake of him to all them that looked for redemption in Jerusalem. And when they had performed all things according to the law of the Lord, they returned into Galilee, to their own city Nazareth. And the child grew, and waxed strong in spirit, filled with wisdom: and the grace of God was upon him.

Christmas Carols

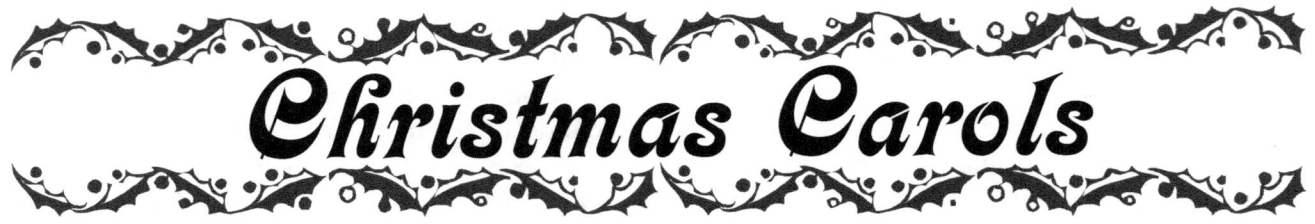

Sing the two Christmas Carols together as a family. Discuss what the songs mean.

God Rest Ye, Merry Gentlemen

D. M. Craik. L. H. Redner, 1865.

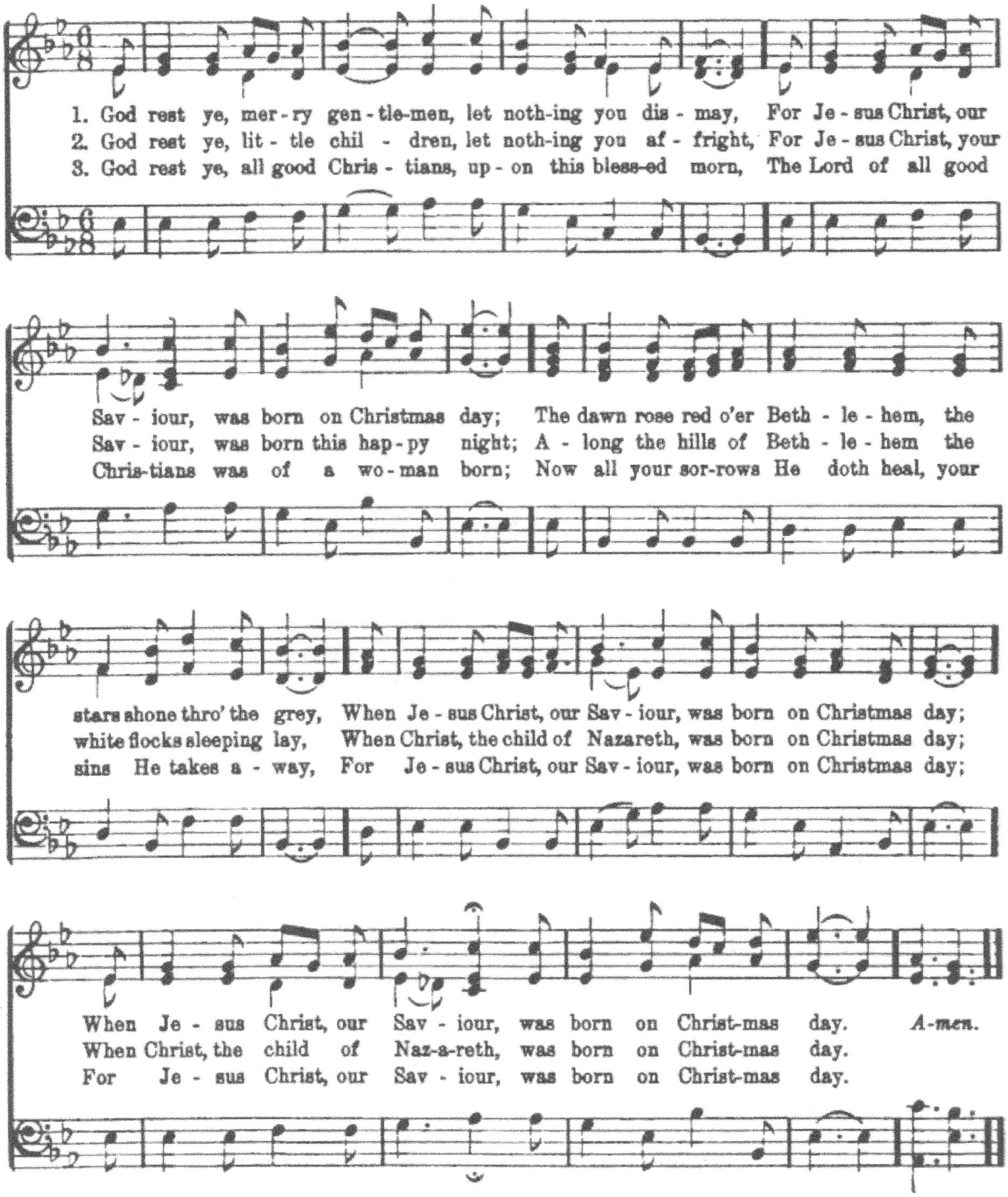
1. God rest ye, mer-ry gen-tle-men, let noth-ing you dis-may, For Je-sus Christ, our
2. God rest ye, lit-tle chil-dren, let noth-ing you af-fright, For Je-sus Christ, your
3. God rest ye, all good Chris-tians, up-on this bless-ed morn, The Lord of all good
Sav-iour, was born on Christmas day; The dawn rose red o'er Beth-le-hem, the
Sav-iour, was born this hap-py night; A-long the hills of Beth-le-hem the
Chris-tians was of a wo-man born; Now all your sor-rows He doth heal, your
stars shone thro' the grey, When Je-sus Christ, our Sav-iour, was born on Christmas day;
white flocks sleeping lay, When Christ, the child of Nazareth, was born on Christmas day;
sins He takes a-way, For Je-sus Christ, our Sav-iour, was born on Christmas day;
When Je-sus Christ, our Sav-iour, was born on Christ-mas day. A-men.
When Christ, the child of Naz-a-reth, was born on Christ-mas day.
For Je-sus Christ, our Sav-iour, was born on Christ-mas day.

Oh Come, Oh Come, Emmanuel

ANON. (Latin, c. 12th Cent.)
Tr. J. M. NEALE, 1851.

H. CAREY, 1723.

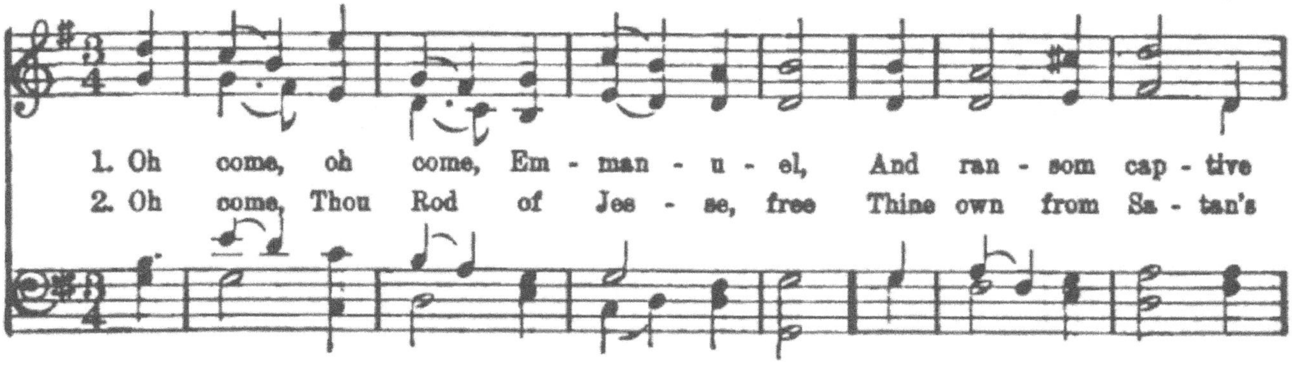

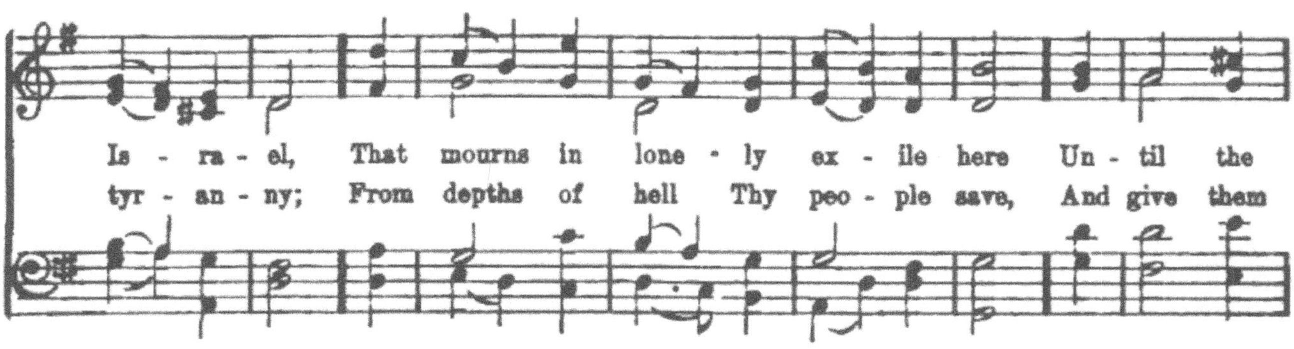

1. Oh come, oh come, Emmanuel, And ransom captive Israel, That mourns in lonely exile here Until the Son of God appear. Rejoice! Rejoice! Emmanuel Shall come to thee, O Israel. Amen.

2. Oh come, Thou Rod of Jesse, free Thine own from Satan's tyranny; From depths of hell Thy people save, And give them vict'ry o'er the grave. Rejoice! Rejoice! Emmanuel Shall come to thee, O Israel.

3. Oh come, Thou Day-Spring, come and cheer
Our spirits by Thine advent here;
Disperse the gloomy clouds of night,
And death's dark shadows put to flight.
    Rejoice! Rejoice! Emmanuel
    Shall come to thee, O Israel.

4. Oh come, Thou Key of David, come,
And open wide our heavenly home;
Make safe the way that leads on high,
And close the path to misery.
    Rejoice! Rejoice! Emmanuel
    Shall come to thee, O Israel.

Index

Authors
- Alcott, Louisa May, 3
- Alden, Raymond MacDonald, 39
- Andersen, Hans Christian, 8
- Bailey, Carolyn Sherwin, 83
- Bible, 132, 136, 140, 144
- Chambers, Robert, 35
- Field, Eugene, 115
- Gaskell, Elizabeth, 62, 68
- Gladden, Washington, 120, 126
- Harkison, Elizabeth, 89
- Howells, W.D., 44
- Kingsley, Florence M., 16
- Luke, 140, 144
- Matthew, 136
- Nesbit, E., 20, 27
- Puetz, Amy, 51, 74
- Robinson, Anna, 56
- Sidney, Margaret, 94, 101

"Away in a Manger" (carol), 92
Babouscka, Adapted from a Russian Tale, 109
Beans are Hot (game), 38
"Becky's Christmas Dream" by Alcott, 3
Bill of Fare for a Christmas Dinner by H.H., 113
"Birth of Jesus" Matthew 1:17-2:23, 136
Blind-Man's Buff (game), 7
Bread Pudding (recipe), 25
Butterscotch (recipe), 55
Buz (game), 100
Carols
- "Away in a Manger", 92
- "Deck the Hall with Boughs of Holly", 107
- "God Rest Ye, Merry Gentlemen", 146
- "Hark! The Herald Angels Sing", 34
- "I Heard the Bells on Christmas Day", 124
- "It Came Upon the Midnight Clear", 125
- "Joy to the World!", 61
- "O Come, All Ye Faithful", 33
- "O Little Town of Bethlehem", 60
- "Oh Come, Oh Come, Emmanuel", 147
- "Silent Night", 108
- "We Three Kings of Orient Are", 93

Charles Dickens, 7, 13, 106, 135, 143
"Christ is Born" Luke 2, 144
Christmas (meaning of the word), 72
"Christmas Bells!" by Margaret Sidney, 101
Christmas Carol Wall Hanging (craft), 139
Christmas celebration in other countries, 37
Christmas Chuckles, 32
Christmas Cookies (recipe), 131
"Christmas Every Day" by W.D. Howells, 44
"Christmas Far From Home" by Amy Puetz Fox, 74
"Christmas Joy," 123
Christmas Play, 67
"Christmas Storms and Sunshine" by Gaskell, 62, 68
"Christmas Story, The" Luke 1, 140
Christmas Traditions, Origin of Stockings, 42
"Coming Messiah, The" From the Bible, 132
"Conscience-Pudding, The" by E. Nesbit, 20, 27
Contradiction, (game) 135
Cooking, 25, 55, 131
Crafts, 14, 50, 88, 111, 139
"Deck the Hall with Boughs of Holly" (carol), 107
Dickens, Charles. See Charles Dickens.

Earth, Air, Fire, and Water (game), 73
Even or Odd? (game), 38
"First Christmas Tree, The" by Eugene Field, 115
"Fir-Tree, The" by Hans Christian Andersen, 8
Fudge (recipe), 55
Games, 7, 38, 72-73, 100, 135
"Getting a Christmas for the Little Ones" by Sidney, 94
Gingerbread Men Cookies (recipe), 131
"God Rest Ye, Merry Gentlemen" (carol), 146
"Hark! The Herald Angels Sing" (carol), 34
How, When, and Where (game), 135
Hunt the Slipper (game), 7
"I Heard the Bells on Christmas Day" (carol), 124
"It Came Upon the Midnight Clear" (carol), 125
"Joy to the World!" (carol), 61
Lanterns (craft), 88
"Legend of Babouscka, The", 109
Little Box Ornaments (craft), 14
Meaning of the word "Christmas," 72
Musical Chairs (game), 100
Newspaper, 78
"O Come, All Ye Faithful" (carol), 33
"O Little Town of Bethlehem" (carol), 60
"Oh Come, Oh Come, Emmanuel" (carol), 147
Paper Chains (craft), 111
Parisian Sweets (recipe), 55
"Paulina's Christmas" by Anna Robinson, 56
Picture-Frame (craft), 111
Plain Bread Pudding (recipe), 25
Play (Christmas), 67
Plum Pudding (recipe), 25
Poems
- "Birth of Christ, The" by Tennyson, 130
- "Candlemas Dialogue, A" by Rossetti, 49
- "Blest Feast of the Nativity!" by W. F. D., 26
- "Christmas Carol, A" by Rossetti, 66
- "Christmas Carol for Children, A" by Luther, 6
- "Christmas Day" by Christina Rossetti, 134
- "Christmas Greeting, A," 53
- "Christmas Spirit, The" by Hugh Hume, 138
- "Good King Wenceslas" by Neale, 54
- "Love Came Down" by Rossetti, 110
- "Merry Christmas, A" by Havergal, 2
- "Time Flies: A Reading Diary" by Rossetti, 59
- "While Shepherds Watched" by Tate, 118

Puss in the Corner (game), 72-73
Quiz, 19, 143
Recipes. See Cooking.
Remembering Those Far Away, 112
Riddles, 43, 119
"Saint Nicholas" Adapted by Amy Puetz Fox, 35
Scrap-Bag, A (craft), 50
"Shepherd's Story, The" by Washington Gladden, 120, 126
"Silent Night" (carol), 108
Simple Bill of Fare for a Christmas Dinner, 113
"Star, The" by Florence M. Kingsley, 16
"Story of the Christ-Child, A" by Elizabeth Harkison, 89
"Trusty's Christmas" by Carolyn Sherwin Bailey, 83
12 Days of Christmas by John Rodemeyer, 87
Vanilla Pudding (recipe), 26
Walnut-Shell Turtle, A (craft), 50
"Wenceslas" by Amy Puetz Fox, 51
"We Three Kings of Orient Are" (carol), 93
"Why the Chimes Rang" by Alden, 39

www.ingramcontent.com/pod-product-compliance
Lightning Source LLC
LaVergne TN
LVHW081536060526
838200LV00048B/2095